"What maintains the grip of painful patterns that play out again and again in our relationships? *The Power of Attachment* answers that big question and shows why liberating change is possible. Diane Poole Heller is a superb guide for finding your way in the deep, compelling domain of attachment, and her warmth creates a healing connection with the reader."

BRUCE ECKER, MA, LMFT
co-creator of Coherence Therapy and co-author of
Unlocking the Emotional Brain

"*The Power of Attachment* is a beautifully written book, exploring the definitions and manifestations of attachment styles from a strengths-based perspective. Diane's warm and optimistic voice continually empowers the reader to reaccess and strengthen their capacity for secure attachments and to heal relational wounds. Powerful creative exercises, guided imagery, and concrete strategies help the reader to be more internally resourced while deepening their ability to forge secure relationships through repair, empathy, corrective experiences, and compassion. For anyone who works with traumatized clients or has experienced attachment wounds firsthand, this book is a gift—nurturing, enlightening, and healing."

LISA FERENTZ, LCSW-C, DAPA
author of *Finding Your Ruby Slippers:
Transformative Life Lessons from the Therapist's Couch*

"*The Power of Attachment* is a masterful compendium of how to understand and bring healing to the major attachment styles. Equally valuable for both therapists and the general public, this book possesses comprehensive modes of assessment and countless, evolved, effective exercises. Kudos to Dr. Poole Heller for her book that both explores the brain and engages the heart."

DAVID GRAND, PHD
author of *Brainspotting: The Revolutionary New
Therapy for Rapid and Effective Change*

"Diane Poole Heller proves herself a superb guide to the new exciting science of attachment theory. In clear, readable, touching prose, *The Power of Attachment* gives you the practical tools you need to understand yourself and your partner at the deepest level. It has the power to change your life."
TERRENCE REAL, LICSW
founder of the Relational Life Institute
and author of *The New Rules of Marriage:
What You Need to Know to Make Love Work*

"We blame ourselves or our partners when intimacy goes south without awareness of the unconscious relationship template that organizes those failures. With clear illustrations and practical exercises, Diane Poole Heller helps you understand and change this powerful inner operating system that came from your childhood attachment history, thereby defusing the mines in the minefields that love has been for most of us."
RICHARD SCHWARTZ, PHD
founder of the Internal Family Systems method and
author of *You Are the One You've Been Waiting For*

PRAISE FOR *THE POWER OF ATTACHMENT*

"Filled with wise guidance based on decades of clinical experience and scientific training, Dr. Poole Heller provides a wealth of clear, practical tools that anyone can use to improve their relationships and enrich their lives. With warmth, honesty, and a gift for teaching, she weaves together insights from attachment research, neurobiology, and life experience to provide easy-to-use tools to connect more deeply to others and heal our hearts and minds in the process — creating a valuable resource for us all."

RONALD D. SIEGEL, PSYD
assistant professor of psychology at Harvard
Medical School and author of *The Mindfulness Solution:
Everyday Practices for Everyday Problems*

"In *The Power of Attachment,* Diane Poole Heller fearlessly and compassionately explores our innate capacities for truly enriching relationships and the tragedies and terrors that can derail them. Diane's clinical expertise in attachment and trauma guides the reader through many exercises that radically and effectively transform the early perceptions of broken connections into new experiences of genuinely fulfilling, resonant connections. The science is solid; the stories are compelling; the style is engaging; the wisdom is a tremendous gift."

LINDA GRAHAM, MFT
author of *Resilience: Powerful Practices for Bouncing Back
from Disappointment, Difficulty, and Even Disaster*

"Diane Poole Heller has written a gem of a book that clearly conveys what decades of attachment research have taught us about how we become who we are and how we can change. Drawing on her experiences as a person, therapist, and student of psychological science, Heller offers the reader a wealth of insight. The book is a gift — practical and, yes, inspirational — from a very special writer whose depth of understanding, compassion, and humanity shine through on every page."

DAVID WALLIN, PHD
author of *Attachment in Psychotherapy*

"Written with great warmth and clarity, this beautiful book turns the scientific insights of attachment theory into practical healing and help for our most important relationships. It is full of examples, experiential exercises, and deep insights into the lingering effects of childhood. Dr. Heller has a depth of heart, intellect, and experience that is rare and remarkable, and it shows on every page."

RICK HANSON, PHD
author of *Resilient: How to Grow an Unshakable Core of Calm, Strength, and Happiness*

"Diane Poole Heller brings us good news—a healthy romantic relationship is attainable, despite whatever attachment wounds we've survived. Reading this book can be the first step to your own recovery and ability to connect intimately with another. Diane Poole Heller's knowledge of trauma and recovery begins with her own hard-won experience, shared here as the inspiration for her life's work. Whether clinician or client, yoga therapist or student, *The Power of Attachment* is an essential read and reference. Keep this book within easy reach for the moments you fall away from your own sense of compassionate connection. The exercises here helped me grow in love and understanding of my own and my partner's attachment styles and brought us to a new level of intimacy."

AMY WEINTRAUB
founder of LifeForce Yoga, author of
Yoga Skills for Therapists and *Yoga for Depression*

"Diane Poole Heller has given us a new primer on attachment theory that breaks down some basic concepts for readers. She describes the characteristics of the various attachment styles and gives readers some elementary ways to begin to track their own behaviors and skills. The chapter specifically devoted to understanding attachment in relationships can serve as a good introduction for couples or anyone interested in coupling. Diane's warm and personal writing style makes this an easy read."

STAN TATKIN, PSYD, MFT
developer of A Psychobiological Approach to
Couple Therapy® (PACT) and author of *Wired for Love:
How Understanding Your Partner's Brain and Attachment Style
Can Help You Defuse Conflict and Build a Secure Relationship*

THE
POWER OF
ATTACHMENT

ALSO BY DIANE POOLE HELLER

Books

Crash Course: A Self-Healing Guide to Auto Accident Trauma and Recovery (with Laurence Heller)

Audio Programs

Healing Your Attachment Wounds: How to Create Deep and Lasting Intimate Relationships

Online Programs

Therapy Mastermind Circle

Attachment Mastery Program

Attachment in Adult Relationships

Unraveling the Mystery of Memory in the Treatment of Trauma (with Peter Levine)

Secure Attachment Parenting in the Digital Age (with Kim John Payne)

DVD Programs

Auto Accident Recovery Program

Character Structure: From Trauma to Transformation

Dynamic Attachment Re-parenting experience (DARe):
DARe Module 1: Healing Early Attachment Wounds and Embracing the Authentic Self
DARe Module 2: Creating Healthy Adult Relationships
DARe Module 3: The Neurobiology of Loving Relationships
DARe Module 4: From Wound to Wellness: Excavating Core Intactness, Power and Resiliency

Healing the Divine Wound, Unveiling the Sacred Heart

Enlivening Intimacy, Sensuality, and Sexuality

THE
POWER OF
ATTACHMENT

How to Create
Deep and Lasting
Intimate Relationships

DIANE POOLE HELLER, PhD

sounds true
BOULDER, COLORADO

Sounds True
Boulder, CO 80306

Published 2019

Cover design by Tara DeAngelis
Book design by Beth Skelley

Printed in Canada

Library of Congress Cataloging-in-Publication Data

Names: Heller, Diane Poole, author.
Title: The power of attachment : how to create deep and lasting intimate
    relationships / Diane Poole Heller, PHD.
Description: Boulder, CO : Sounds True, [2019] | Includes bibliographical
    references and index.
Identifiers: LCCN 2018031640 (print) | LCCN 2018037737 (ebook) |
    ISBN 9781622038268 (ebook) | ISBN 9781622038251 (pbk.)
Subjects: LCSH: Attachment behavior. | Interpersonal relations.
Classification: LCC BF575.A86 (ebook) | LCC BF575.A86 H45 2019 (print) |
    DDC 155.5/1241—dc23
LC record available at https://lccn.loc.gov/2018031640

10 9 8 7 6 5 4 3 2

To all those who have the courage
to dive the depths,
live the truth of their story,
feel compassion for the pain,
and share the wisdoms gained.

CONTENTS

FOREWORD

Within every person, there exists the weight and opportunity of a hero's journey. I believe this, and have seen it validated thousands of times in my forty-five years of clinical experience. Many of our life's decisions are fueled by our ability to hold (or not hold) ourselves to this wholly unique vision of who we each strive to be.

The hero in all of us is faced with an externalized threat or dilemma: a powerful foe. This foe, in our lives, is a symbolic obstacle to inner order, peace, love, prosperity, relationship, and the greater good. This inner foe seems overwhelming in its strength and power. It seeks to destroy the hero, as well as punish and spread a dark cloud.

Trauma has obvious parallels to the foe. At its core, trauma (and deep emotional wounding) is about overwhelm and helplessness. It inhibits our vitality, dulls our senses, and weakens us by separating us from each other through the grip of fear and suffering. Separation from each other is one of the most effective ways to undermine a relationship and even a civilization. There is also an allegorical relationship between the torment of civilization and the torment of the self: terror annihilates our connection to ourselves, to the embodied self, to what is true and eternal in us. We become isolated and adrift. We no longer head outside the door to water our gardens, and in the process lose the gifts of nourishment.

If trauma is the foe, then attachment to self and others would be the inner task of the hero. It describes where the hero comes from, and also commands a path that must be taken. Heroes aren't born, they are cultivated through meeting adversity. The most compelling heroes of ancient lore are the ones who suffer great disappointments and loss. They aren't ready for the task at hand. They fail at first. They change. They prove themselves to others and to themselves. They earn the support of friends and allies. They persevere. They find their own mastery. They triumph.

Mythology aside, in real everyday life, our connection to the role of our inner hero is more sporadic. We are not meant to always embody the role of the hero. Embodying the role of hero can even leave us vulnerable to those who would take advantage of our benevolent intents. The business of media oftentimes distorts and corrupts our faith in heroes. In these contemporary times, myth has become a rare commodity.

In the context of developing a connection to the self, of finding safety and security in ourselves and in others, in moving through our daily tasks (from the minute and mundane to the "macro" decisions of love, career, family, friends, and residence), it is edifying to make contact with our "heightened selves" in an embodied and present way to guide our choices and actions.

This brings us back around to the topic of attachment, as attachment is about connection. Attachment not only describes *how* we contact and connect with others, but also with ourselves and with our bodies. That is why understanding how trauma impacts our tissues and our nervous systems, and thereby our sense of safety, is so vitally critical to navigating the complexities of our attachment patterns.

Our bodies generate vast surges of survival energy (to run, pounce, kick, slash, flee, and destroy—or to attach) when we are under perceived threat. If circumstances leave us stuck in this charged state for too long, it is as if a circuit breaker cuts off our power, a life-saving adaptation rescuing us from too much threat too fast (or too little support for too long). In other words, we dissociate. The same life-saving energy mobilizations that allow us to fend off or escape threat stays trapped in our bodies when overwhelmed. This trapped threat-response energy gets caught in a feedback loop: a pointless, destructive, and circular conversation between body and brain. Like pointing a microphone at a speaker, this conversation relentlessly amplifies itself. The brain asks, "Are we okay?" Our body replies, "All I can feel is stress. Aren't we dying?" The brain figures, "I guess we are dying then. We must need to work harder."

Our physiology convinces us of our emotions. The very foundation of a healthy psyche and body—our capacity to feel *safe*—is undermined by the foe of trauma. If our bodies are stuck in survival mode, our emotions and feelings will turn our attentions obsessively toward seeking safety. This inhibits our vitality, and so we will avoid risk. All incoming experiences tend to take on a quality of threat, which undermines our capacity to make contact with others.

The bad news is that trauma is a fact of life, but (and this is the good news) it doesn't have to be a life sentence. What I have taught to thousands of clients and students over the years is that the key in taming this vast sea of distress involves learning how to touch into small chunks of the experience (including body sensations, feelings, images, thoughts, and energies) and encountering tiny little bits piecemeal, one by one. These form small islands of safety in a raging see of trauma. And then these islands begin to connect, and little by little there forms a solid mass of (relative) safety—a place where we can stand back and observe these difficult sensations and haunting feelings, and then slowly come to peace with them.

The essential questions become: "How much can I feel while staying present in the here and now?" "How much can I tolerate before I check out?" and "What can I do to stay within my range of tolerance?" The wisdom of our bodies provides the answers to how we may carve out a protected space in the roiling currents of terror, fear, and helplessness—a small haven of safety that gives us enough time to explore that titrated chunk of experience, consider it, take it apart, keep what is valuable, and discard what is not. In this way, we gradually change the message of our physiology from terror to safety. The focus shifts from protection and escape to warmth and connection, from panic or shutdown to exploration and compassion. Our foe is beaten, the danger passes. We come out of our homes and tend to those things that nourish and sustain ourselves, as well as others. There is peace and prosperity in the realm. Life thrives in emotional richness.

Since it is true that all of us have *some* complication with "healthy" attachment, I am thrilled to be introducing you to this book. I have been fortunate in knowing its author, Dr. Heller, for several decades. Diane was one of my brightest students, and someone whom I continue to admire and cherish greatly. Her qualities of warmth, energy, caring, and insight have benefited thousands of her clients and students over the years. Her gifts and wisdom are ever-present throughout *The Power of Attachment*, a book that will provide you with an accessible yet exemplary framework for identifying your own unique, sometimes complex attachment struggles, delivered with Diane's wit and breezy, unpretentious tone. The included exercises will certainly help you rediscover your true, embodied self, and will guide you to renegotiate your own obstacles to connections with others.

It is a book for therapists who work with attachment issues with their clients. It is equally for those of us beginning new relationships, for those wanting to enrich long-term relationships, and for those of us who are ending relationships—and learning and healing from those endings. I am excited for you to begin this engaging journey. May we all heroically overcome our foes and bring wholeness, prosperity, and purpose to civilization, as well as to the Civilization of the Self.

PETER A. LEVINE, PHD
Author of the bestselling *Waking the Tiger: Healing Trauma*,
In an Unspoken Voice: How the Body Releases Trauma and Restores Goodness,
and *Trauma and Memory: Brain and Body in a Search for the Living Past:
A Practical Guide for Understanding and Working with Traumatic Memory*

INTRODUCTION

I want to start by telling you a story about something that happened to me back in 1988 when I was preparing for my wedding. It was only two weeks away, and I was so excited, but also incredibly busy, as people often are just before the *big day*. I was driving around Denver, frantically attending to a myriad of wedding-related errands and details. I was going about fifty-five miles per hour when, out of the corner of my eye, I saw something sliding off my planner toward the car floor. It was a porcelain figurine—one of those bride-and-groom wedding cake toppers—and it had meant a lot to my mother-in-law to give it to me, so I really didn't want it to break. Driving down a traffic-filled Santa Fe Drive, I foolishly unbuckled my seat belt and leaned over to grab the fleeing figurine. When I did, I unintentionally jerked the steering wheel. I swerved head-on into oncoming traffic and smashed into a car coming the opposite way.

The man in the other car was going about as fast as I was. The collision caused his car to jump into the air and land upside down on the street. Luckily, he was in an old Volvo that was built like a tank, so he came away from the accident relatively unscathed. I'll forever be grateful for that.

I wasn't so fortunate. Since my seat belt was off, my body lurched forward, and my head shattered the windshield, giving me a traumatic brain injury. This put a bit of a damper on my upcoming wedding, but I went ahead with it anyway. My head swelled up like a misshapen red basketball, which was bad enough, but then on top of that I suffered from all sorts of unpleasant symptoms. I got numbers mixed up. I started acting strangely. I put the iron in the refrigerator. I left the milk in the microwave. And then there was the time I left my car running all day in the parking garage at work with the keys locked inside. Needless to say, it was a disorienting, frightening, and embarrassing time.

But here's the interesting part: I also began to experience moments of incredible bliss. Here and there, I had these fascinating states of expansion. I could see and feel things way beyond my regular, everyday perception. And throughout it all, I felt quite tender and openhearted. I saw the best in others as if it naturally emanated from their very core. These wonderful experiences lasted about six weeks or so, and during that time it seemed like I received a tremendous download of compassion and understanding.

Unfortunately, that expansiveness also excavated some unexpected and difficult experiences. I took a turn in a negative direction, abruptly, as if falling down an elevator shaft directly into the dark night of the soul. In fact, I struggled quite a bit for the next three or four years. The crash had triggered memories of my childhood—a history of trauma that I had long been dissociated from. I floundered in my attempts to integrate all the disparate highs and lows I was experiencing. Apparently, all of this—particularly recalling traumatic memories—happens to a lot of people who survive high-impact accidents.

I did everything I could think of to make sense of what was happening to me. I looked up various professionals in the Yellow Pages (for those of you who remember using the Yellow Pages) and interviewed them. I gave all sorts of therapies a try. I read everything I could find on trauma and recovery. I attended countless lectures and workshops. Basically, I went on a nationwide search to find anyone who could help me. But nothing worked very well. I found tidbits here and there and tried to stitch them together, but nothing brought me the understanding and relief I needed.

Then I came across Peter Levine and attended one of his Somatic Experiencing (SE) workshops. At the time, I couldn't make much sense out of what Peter was doing, but I knew it had to do with returning the nervous system to regulation. More importantly, I knew right away that SE worked for me. With Peter's help, I slowly recovered and began to appreciate the relationship between physiology and trauma. I learned ways to effectively work with my nervous system and how to reduce the intensity of certain trauma symptoms, and I gained plenty of methods to unpack and integrate extreme experiences. Peter's SE work remains immensely informative and helpful to me.

As I was healing, I decided to study under Peter, becoming one of the first Somatic Experiencing facilitators. I had the much-appreciated opportunity to teach SE worldwide for more than twenty-five years. I learned so much about working with autonomic nervous system regulation, how symptoms bind excess arousal from overwhelming life events, how to evoke and complete unfinished or inhibited self-protective responses, and so much more. I am forever grateful.

Over time, I began to focus on how to reconnect in relationship in the face of the isolation and dissociation that can accompany traumatic experiences, and with Peter's help—and the hard-won lessons of my own recovery—I've been able to meet and work with people in some incredibly dark places. I've helped them to diminish the intensity of their symptoms, enhance their resiliency, and often actually recover completely. It's a genuine privilege to travel on this journey with others and watch as they begin to enjoy their life again. This has become my life's work, and I plan to spend the rest of my life exploring the issues of trauma and resiliency and helping people recover their aliveness and well-being. Here are the major topics and questions I keep coming back to in my work:

- How do we heal broken connections to ourself and others, and how can we come back to a sense of wholeness?

- How do we integrate our diverse experiences and all the parts of ourself that feel so broken and fragmented?

- How do we emerge from incredible loss, fear, and powerlessness to regain empowerment and resiliency?

- When trauma robs us of our physical self through dissociation or loss of boundaries, how do we become embodied and safely connected again?

- How do we reclaim our birthright to feel grounded and centered, to feel connection and compassion, to have access to all the facets of our humanness and our spiritual nature?

I've learned that one key to answering these questions can be found by compassionately understanding our own (and others') early relationship templates, then applying interventions and/or creating relevant corrective experiences related to putting attachment theory into action. Understanding the value of attachment theory in couple's work, individual healing in therapy, and between willing partners or parents who are open to its wisdom is truly revolutionary and incredibly effective.

This book is meant to help you answer some of these questions by uncovering your own early attachment history, understanding the various attachment styles, and focusing on practical approaches toward healing attachment wounds. It's a deep dive into our human capacity for true, enriching connection. Specifically, we will look at how attachment wounds affect our adult relationships and how we can increase our ability to enjoy secure attachment, no matter what type of childhood experiences we may have enjoyed or endured. Through this work, you'll learn what it takes to create deep and lasting intimate relationships.

••

Let's face it: life is sometimes quite hard. It doesn't matter who you are; all of us inevitably bump into challenges and hardships that are beyond our control. If you're on this planet long enough, you're going to be hit with some form of misattunement or loss or abuse or divorce or disease or a car accident or an environmental disaster or war or who knows what. Sometimes these events are so overwhelming that we don't even have the capacity to react or respond to them. You can't stop these things from happening; they're just part of what it means to be human. And to make matters even trickier, epigenetic studies now suggest that—in a manner of speaking—we may inherit the struggles of our ancestors. In one way or another, we're affected by everything that our grandparents, great-grandparents, and so on went through and suffered from. But we're also the products of their resiliency. Throughout time and our evolution as a species, people have been experiencing hardships and doing their best to endure and survive them.

So, life is hard, and it isn't your fault. That's just the way it is, which means that you can stop blaming yourself as if you alone are responsible. There are countless ways for any of us to end up experiencing trauma, and most of them have nothing to do with how we live our life or what kind of person we are. That's the bad news.

But there's good news, too. We can do something about it. We're all born with an amazing capacity to survive, heal, and thrive, which is precisely the reason we've made it this far to begin with. It's what we're built for.

Before we go on, I want to be clear about what I mean when I say the word *trauma*. Without getting too technical, trauma is what results from experiencing an event over which you have little control; sometimes—as in the case with major accidents—you don't even have time to brace yourself for the impact. These events overwhelm your ability to function normally, and this can make you lose trust in your feelings, thoughts, and even your body. In this way, trauma is a form of tremendous fear, loss of control, and profound helplessness.

I've also started thinking of trauma in terms of connection. The theme of *broken connection* has come up in my work repeatedly over the years: broken connection to our body; broken connection to our sense of self; broken connection to others, especially those we love; broken connection to feeling centered or grounded on the planet; broken connection to God, Source, Life Force, well-being, or however we might describe or relate to our inherent sense of spirituality, open-hearted awareness, and beingness. This theme has been so prominent in my work that broken connection and trauma have become almost synonymous to me.

When trauma hits us or we've experienced a lot of relational wounding, we can feel like we're utterly *dis*connected—like we're a tiny little *me* who's isolated and all alone, as if we're in our own little bubble floating around in a sea of distress, cut off from everyone and everything. I think it's our work to pop that imaginary bubble, or at least to build bridges that connect us to others we care about. Unresolved trauma, in my opinion, has led to a nationwide epidemic of loneliness and hurt. And it isn't just in our country. The evidence of this type of pain worldwide is readily available any time you turn on the news. That's not the whole story, fortunately. We can heal and change. All of us are capable of healing and repairing these severed connections: to ourself, other people, the planet, and whatever it is that holds it all together.

But we can't do it alone. First of all, we not capable of healing in isolation. We *need* other people. Stan Tatkin, clinical psychologist, author, speaker, and developer of A Psychobiological Approach to Couple Therapy (PACT) along with his wife, Tracey Boldemann-Tatkin, says that we are hurt in relationship and we heal in relationship.[1] The presence of those close to us makes a difference even in the most dire circumstances. Just to mention one study among thousands, a hospital in Illinois recently demonstrated that coma patients recovered more quickly when they were able to hear the voices of their family members.[2] Like it or not, we're all on this crazy and amazing human journey together.

Our culture might encourage us to think of ourself as do-it-yourself projects, but we get more positive results when we adopt a *we-can-do-it-together* approach. Doing so allows us to foster a healthy relational space with our friends, kids, partners, parents, siblings, and everyone else we contact—even strangers.

Another study I find interesting measured physiological responses in people who were about to climb a steep incline. Their threat responses were highest when they were alone, much lower when accompanied by a stranger, and almost nonexistent when they went with someone they felt connected to.[3] And there are countless other studies to support the same conclusion: our brain and nervous system are not isolated, but interconnected and social. At our core, we are social beings who regulate through connection with others.

We engage in self-regulation too, of course, and learning how to take care of ourself throughout our lifetime is incredibly important. But in this book, we're specifically concerned with how the nervous system initially develops. Ideally, kids grow up with caregivers who serve as "master regulators" of the household.[4] The parents regulate themselves, and they regulate each other as a couple and as a parenting team. And better yet, the parents generate an environment of regulation in the home that benefits everyone involved, especially the children. The type of regulating environment we receive as young children influences how we see the world and interact with others for our entire life. For example, if we're held, nursed, and rocked in a positive way that makes our infant body more alive or relaxed or comfortable—by someone who's regulated, attentive, and loving—those qualities and that regulatory impact get imprinted into our nervous system and body through implicit, nonconscious memory.

Our nervous system learns to co-regulate in this manner by receiving information directly from caregivers, and that regulation becomes who we are on a neurological level. We need skin-to-skin contact, loving gazes and smiles, and heartbeat-to-heartbeat rhythmic communication. Unfortunately, we're also easily influenced at an early age by less-than-ideal circumstances. If you didn't grow up with the type of compassionate exchange I just described, your nervous system has a gap where that interactive regulation should be, making it more difficult as you age to trust others, ask others for help, or even *think* of asking for help when you need it. When attachment is disturbed, a child often won't have proximity-seeking behaviors they need to keep them safe. As it turns out, we can be a lot more autonomous when we rely on a support system. Doing so enables us to acquire the social and life skills we need, practice them, and eventually try them out in the world as we explore and manifest our gifts. Spending time alone is incredibly important for many of us, but too often we hold back with others and the world out of fear of criticism, rejection, shame, humiliation, or simply because we're afraid of making mistakes. I once heard a public speaker say, "I've learned so much from my mistakes; I think it's a great idea to go out into the world and make some more!"

Self-regulation and co-regulation are both needed and beneficial throughout our lifetime. Many of us have established techniques to regulate our own nervous system—yoga, breathing practices, physical exercise, and meditation—and I don't want to diminish the importance of how helpful those can be. Being comfortable in your own skin and having tools that help you relax is a really big deal, but learning how to feel safe with others is revolutionary. When your nervous system can co-regulate with other people, and you feel safe and playful and relaxed, you can develop a stronger sense of secure attachment and enjoy its profound rewards, no matter what environment you grew up in. So I focus on *being with others* as a type of "co-mindfulness." We include others in our meditation, our practice, and our overall path to healing, and at the same time, they include us in theirs. Results vary, of course, but the research indicates that we all do better when we're doing it together.

In order to heal together, we need to feel safe. Especially in intimate relationships, experiencing a sense of threat is counterproductive to resolving issues (not to mention undesirable in other ways). When we feel threatened, it becomes increasingly difficult to access the parts of our brain that are oriented toward self-awareness and devoted to connecting to others. Keep all of this in mind as we move forward together. Seek to feel safe in your relationships and remember to help others feel the same. Be open to new ways to heal and regulate—both by yourself and with others—and it will foster greater connection and promote transformational intimacy.

As you'll discover, this is a hands-on book. It's full of suggestions and exercises, so I want to offer this short visualization practice to get us started.

EXERCISE   Who Helps You Feel Safe and Relaxed?

Take a moment to think about anyone in your life with whom you feel safe and relaxed. Maybe it's your spouse, significant other, parent, grandparent, friend, child, therapist, or a stranger you met in a workshop. It could even be your favorite pet. Whoever it is, you can really find your feet with them and feel truly comfortable. You don't need to visualize everyone who comes to mind—just choose one or two—and if no one seems to fit this description, that's okay too; I'll talk later about what to do if this is the case. But if someone does come to mind right now, picture them in as much detail as you can. Feel what it's like to be with them. What sensations come up for you? Where do you feel them in your body? Take a few minutes to try this exercise on and sink into whatever sense of presence and relaxation arises.

Let's go back a couple of paragraphs to the positive co-regulation situation I described—the one in which a baby is held in a beneficial, loving way. In this ideal scenario (which far too few of us experience), the child grows up in a prosocial family—one that values protection, presence, play, consistency, and responsiveness. Whenever the baby coos or reaches out or looks into their caregivers' faces, those faces look back at the child in a way that lets them know they're special. The love is palpable. The caregivers cuddle the child, play with those cute little fingers and toes, and touch them in a way that the child knows on a fundamental level that they are safe. And from a very young age, the child knows that they have some influence on the world because when they cry out, something good happens. Before they even have the words to express basic needs and feelings, someone responds—whether a mother or father or someone else—and the child comes to rely on a consistent, loving presence that tries to understand them and meet their needs.

And in a truly ideal situation, this gets even better. Not only do the caregivers protect the child, but they're also there when the child doesn't behave or feel or speak in the most optimal ways. No matter what comes up in the child's experience—happiness, distress, confusion, excitement, or anger—their parents are there throughout it all, consistently, in a present, responsive, and loving way.

I call this the *ideal* situation, of course, because this is what our childhood is supposed to look like. This is how we grow up with secure attachment, which John Bowlby—one of the pioneers of attachment theory—suggests we're biologically designed for. We're actually pre-programmed to create and maintain attachments with others. For all social mammals—including humans—evolution has fashioned us in such a way to keep us together and safe until we're ready to go out on our own and further the cycle with our own children, who will foster secure attachment in their own children in turn. As we know, this often doesn't go as planned. However, beneath the scars and maladapted behaviors, we all have this attachment system that's oriented to trust and togetherness with loved ones. And the more we encounter an ideal situation like the one described, the more our inherent design for secure attachment will flourish. It actually gets constructed in an embodied, somatic way that shapes our nervous system, brain, and even our muscles and tissues.

There's a term I want to introduce here called *contingency*, which means something a little different from how it might sound. In this context, *contingency* refers to a relational experience in which you feel understood by another person. You have a felt sense that this person is attuned to you, that they resonate with who you are. You feel they "get" you. You *get gotten* and *feel felt*, so to speak. When you tell them a story or something about an experience you've had, you feel they meet you in an emotional and even spiritual way. It's a deep sense of connection. It doesn't happen enough, of course, because a lot of the time when we speak or listen to others, we don't pay enough attention or dig deep enough to empower this sense of contingency to happen. As an important side note, one way to generate contingency is to ask clarifying questions when others are speaking to you. Relevant questions show that we're really listening and care to comprehend the other person thoroughly.

When we're newborns, we don't have many ways to express ourself other than crying. Sometimes we cry because we have an obvious need—say, we're hungry or need a diaper change. But babies also cry to communicate other needs. An ideal parent or caregiver will pay attention to these cries and try to decipher what each cry means. Sometimes it means the baby needs a nap; sometimes the baby wants to be picked up and held; sometimes it means the baby wants to be left alone. But the main point here is that the parent is trying to understand, to *get* what's going on with the child. And this allows the child to feel safe and relaxed, especially if there is a need that the parent can meet.

Dan Siegel, clinical professor of psychiatry and founding co-director of the Mindful Awareness Research Center at UCLA, says that we're "natural born contingency detectors."[5] We instinctively know when someone gets us and when they don't. Our brain is finely attuned to this; it's hypersensitive to inconsistencies and authenticity. For example, you've undoubtedly experienced times when you tell someone a vulnerable personal story and they respond with something like, "Uh-huh, I get it. I know where you're coming from," but you can tell that they don't. They might believe that they understand you, but you can tell they don't quite get you. Isn't it amazing that we can make such a distinction? We grow up with this felt sense of when people get us and when they don't. That's remarkable to me.

In our adult relationships, it seems like we should have a lot more going for us than babies do because we have all of these words to use. Unfortunately, we're not as good at articulating our needs or understanding others as we think we are. Sometimes, we misunderstand each other, and in addition to feeling misattuned, we can feel alienated, shamed, or attacked, or we can inadvertently encourage others to feel that way. That's why it's crucial to put the effort into becoming more sensitive to one another and to really "get" what the other person is talking about. For adults, finding contingency is incredibly important. It doesn't matter whether we're sharing a moment of grief, happiness, pain, or pleasure—that sense of attunement and resonance is extremely nourishing.

So much of what seems to be going on in our adult relationships is directly imported from our early attachment history. Understanding this will help us view ourself and others more compassionately because we realize so much of our relationship patterns may be related more to our early upbringing rather than our current partner's shortcomings. For our significant others, we will want to take the time to enter into resonance with them and offer that important experience of contingency. And it's also important to focus on finding at least a few good people who can do the same for us because those are the relationships we want to most invest in. As author and research professor Brené Brown from the University of Houston recommends, we should look for the people who deserve to hear our stories.[6] Brené suggests that there may be only a few people we know who we can trust to hold our stories with respect, who honor our vulnerability, and can meet us authentically in our sharing.

When I discovered just how important contingency is, I performed a bit of a "garage sale" on my relationships. I identified the ones with the most possibility for growth and decided to put more of my energy into those people. On the flip side, I also chose to put less energy into the people who didn't seem to be very supportive or capable of positive empowerment. I'm not suggesting that you do this yourself, but I do encourage you to make sure your support system is strong and nourishing. Take an added interest in people who feel safe, available, and emotionally resonant. Choose your people wisely. This doesn't mean to avoid conflict, but focus on the people with whom you have the possibility of working things out—relationships that can weather the inevitable disagreements and disappointments and eventually become stronger and more resilient as a result. Some now say that *who* you eat your meals with is more important than *what* you eat or *how* you exercise. When it comes to enjoying healthy relationships and growing into your own secure attachment, it truly matters who you surround yourself with in life.

Okay, let's try out this idea in a practical way. This next exercise is a little like the one we did a few pages ago, but it's a tad more specific.

EXERCISE   Recalling Contingency

I want you to call to mind a particular experience in which you felt a meeting of minds or communion of souls—a time when you felt appreciated or understood in an uncommon way. In the last exercise, we focused on particular people, but for this one, I want you to recall the experience itself. Remember just how good it feels to share deep insights with others, to enjoy those rare meetings of minds and souls, to arrive at some felt sense of significant understanding and connection. In *Love 2.0: Finding Happiness and Health in Moments of Connection*, Barbara Fredrickson says that these moments constitute love itself, no matter how long they last or who they occur with.[7] Take as long as you need to remember this type of experience. Embody the feeling as best you can. What was it like to "get gotten" and "feel felt"? What do you most notice emotionally or in your body as you remember? Let that depth of attunement come back to you in all its details. What stands out most to you? Does something new come up that you hadn't thought of before? What was this like for you then, and what's it like for you now?

AN INTRODUCTION TO ATTACHMENT STYLES

The human attachment system is an inherent, biological, and natural process that relates to everything we do in life, especially when it comes to our relationships with others. Although *secure* attachment is what we're after here, it's important to note that whatever attachment style we live with evolved to keep us safe. Even insecure attachment patterns are designed to help us survive dangerous situations, and none of these styles are set in stone. The next four chapters look at each of these four adaptations in depth and provide ways to work with them. Here's a quick overview to get us going:

> **Secure Attachment.** This is the type of attachment in the ideal situation described earlier. Securely attached people typically grew up with plenty of love and support from consistently responsive caregivers, and as adults they are interdependent, connecting with others in healthy, mutually beneficial ways. They are okay both in connection and on their own; they can think with flexibility, can perceive a range of possibilities, are comfortable with differences, and resolve conflicts without much drama. They can internalize the love they feel from others and forgive easily.

> **Avoidant Attachment.** People with this attachment style have a tendency to keep intimacy at arm's length or to diminish the importance of relationships. They often were neglected: left alone too much as children, rejected by their caregivers, or their parents weren't present enough (or only present when teaching them some type of task). Avoidants have disconnected—put the brakes on—their attachment system, so reconnecting to others in safe and healthy ways is extremely important.

> **Ambivalent Attachment.** People with the ambivalence adaptation deal with a lot of anxiety about having their needs met or feeling secure in being loved or lovable.

Their parents might have shown them love, but as children they never knew when their parents might get distracted and utterly pull the rug out from underneath them. Their care was unpredictable or notably intermittent. They can be hypervigilant about relational slights or any hint of abandonment, which amps up their attachment system into overdrive. Anticipating the impending inevitability of abandonment that they are convinced is coming, they often feel sad, disappointed, or angry before anything actually happens in their adult relationships. For ambivalents, consistency and reassurance are paramount.

Disorganized Attachment. This attachment style is characterized by an excess of fear, and the attachment system is at cross purposes with the instinct to survive threat. When stressed, sick, or frightened, a child naturally wants to seek comfort and protection from a loving parent, but what do they do when the same parent is the source of fear or distress? People with this style can get stuck in a threat response and/or swing between avoidance and ambivalence without much of an identifiable pattern. They often suffer from psychological and physical confusion. Disorganized parents may fear their own children. As children, they saw their parents as threatening, or their parents simply emanated an atmosphere of fear or dread due to their own unresolved trauma. Disorganized folks are often emotionally dysregulated, dealing with sudden shifts in arousal, or dissociated and checked out. Since they are prone to the most disturbance, reestablishing a fundamental sense of regulation and relative safety are the most important things for people with this attachment style.

As we review these different attachment styles, I invite you to explore how they line up with your own experience and that of your partner, parents, friends, and children. Try to activate your curiosity about these different dynamics and remain as playful and open as possible. Please also keep in mind that these are not fixed categories and that a person can exhibit a mix of attachment styles. Maybe you can relate to the material on secure attachment, but part of you is avoidant and another part seems ambivalent. Or maybe you're situationally disorganized, becoming markedly afraid under a particular type of stress. I'm sure you're already aware that different relationships bring out different qualities, feelings, and reactions in you. There are a lot of variables to consider, and the goal isn't to shoehorn yourself and others into categories that don't always fit. Rather, the idea is to see that your dominant patterns can become more fluid and manageable. My hope is that the more you understand yourself and these adaptations, the more you'll let go of any lingering patterns of self-criticism and judgment. With compassion, we start wherever we are, work to heal our wounds the best we can, and enhance our secure attachment skills along the way.

And because so much of our interest regarding attachment styles has to do with romantic partnerships, I think it's important to point out that our attachment system is always on and active. When we get to know someone more over time, perhaps while dating, when we depend more on them and they depend more on us, they become our primary attachment figure and vice versa. It takes a while to neurologically recognize someone else as relatively permanent in our lives. We can coast through the early stages of romantic relationships with some degree of euphoria, which can feel magical, energizing, and exciting. Part of what's going on is that we're feeling the rush of the biochemical cocktail that's designed to keep us attracted to the other person. Unfortunately, during this initial part of the relationship, we can miss (and even ignore) some important red flags about our partner. As the saying goes, love is blind. For this reason, I advise not making any huge relational decisions until later, when oxytocin, vasopressin, and other chemicals wear off a bit.

I also invite you to review your past relationships to see how this checks out. After a certain point, did you experience a shift in the perceptions and associations related to your partner? Did something crucial change somewhere between the one- and two-year mark? This phenomenon is not always easy to track because so much that's going on is embodied and largely unconscious, but I think most of us can relate to major changes happening in our relationships after a while, seemingly out of nowhere.

COGNITIVE DEVELOPMENT, BRAIN SCIENCE, AND ATTACHMENT THEORY

Of course, our experiences don't come out of nowhere. To make more sense of how we're deeply influenced by things that happen so early on in our lives, let's take a quick look at some of the science behind how our nervous system and brain work.

In the first stages of life, we soak up everything that happens around us, and we especially bring in constant information from the people in charge of taking care of us. In the first year and a half or so of life, we don't possess the cognitive development it takes to make a story out of any of this data; it's just an ongoing amalgamation of pictures, feelings, events, colors, and sensations that goes not into our conscious memory, but into our *implicit memory*, our "not conscious yet" memory. It's like our body, mind, and soul work together as a perpetual tape recorder that documents everything that happens to us, but when we're at such an impressionable young age, we have no way to play the tape back to make any sense of it. Most people cannot access these very early memories but can clearly detect when they are triggered. We can often track sensations, actions, or gestures that may reveal significant events in our implicit memory and by paying more attention make them explicit, creating more opportunities for growth and healing.

These early experiences live in our implicit memory because at the time of their imprint, our brain hasn't yet fully developed. As we age, we gain more access to the *hippocampus*, a part of the brain located beneath the cerebral cortex that is associated with our awareness of space and time. The hippocampus gradually develops over the first eighteen months or so of our life, but until then, we can't locate an experience in space or place it in the past, present, or future. Both attachment-related memories and trauma-related memories tend to happen in *fast-circuit learning*, in which things happen so quickly in our experience that they bypass the hippocampus altogether. In the case of early attachment-related memories, this process occurs simply because the hippocampus isn't developed yet. With trauma, it happens because the experience is often so overwhelmingly intense and sudden that our nervous system can't cope with it, and the experience often bypasses the higher-functioning parts of the brain that would allow for integration.

Although it takes a while for your hippocampus to develop, your brain comes into this world fairly well prepared. It's born fat, so to speak. It comes with lots of extra cells—extra potential—in case you need them. In this way, the brain is positively inclined because it's set up to take care of any number of possible scenarios. If you grow up in a prosocial family in which people are present, playful, protective, and safe, then your brain prunes away some of the defensive parts of the brain you were born with, emphasizing the more relational aspects instead. This means you become less likely to scan your environment for danger all the time, being chronically hypervigilant and always ready to engage with a *threat response*. In general, you grow up trusting other people and expecting positivity and responsiveness in your relationships. The parts of your brain aligned with secure attachment in this case are highly structured, evolved, and easy to access.

But what happens if you grow up in a less-than-ideal situation? Maybe you're born in a war zone or your parents are addicted or one of them is severely depressed. Or you have a caregiver who is abusive and scary. Or maybe your caregivers have unprocessed trauma and go about life frightened and unavailable. In this case, your brain prunes away the parts aligned with secure attachment and emphasizes its own defensive structures. To manage your situation and respond to the danger in your world, your threat response becomes exaggerated. And this is how our brain gets shaped around our experienced relational environment.

That's practical, of course. You can see the intelligence in that. If you need more protection from others, it's appropriate to develop a radar system that detects the earliest signs of danger. However, it gets tricky later in life when you come across safe, supportive relationships. We all make adaptations as children to whatever relational environment we grow up in. All of that typically isn't conscious but embedded in our bodies, so that's how we relate to others—according to our implicit memory (also called our *procedural memory*), which informs everything we think about the world. This explains why we sometimes behave in certain ways and experience feelings that seem out of place or maladaptive to us. It doesn't matter what stories our *declarative* memory tells us about early personal interactions; if we have a nervous system that was shaped in response to recurring threat, our threat response will be easily triggered later in life, and it's going to take a little work to shift toward secure attachment because of this early sculpting. And when we get really overwhelmed, we can even go into a *freeze response* and become immobile or lose our ability to talk or hear. In this way, trauma has a profound effect on social functioning—our "social engagement," as Stephen Porges, research professor and the developer of the Polyvagal Theory, calls it.[8]

Of course, we need our threat response in everyday life to deal with actual dangers; it's just that we want to tone it down so that it isn't overactive too much of the time. Our goal is to learn how to calm the alarm center in our brain—the *amygdala*—and to activate our *medial prefrontal cortex*, which is what we need to engage in a meaningful way with others.

Rick Hanson, a psychologist, speaker, and author who focuses on neuroscience and mindfulness, points out that our brain is somewhat biased toward fear and threat because the brain's most important job is to keep us safe.[9] We can view that positively, too. And as adults interested in accessing the benefits of secure attachment, this tendency means that we need to put more focus on whatever good comes our way. For this reason, I spend a lot of time working with my clients on corrective experiences, and you'll find many of them in this book.

It doesn't matter whether our nervous system is primed toward threat or toward safety because beneath that original patterning, our brain is designed with *neuroplasticity*. In other words, it is constructed to allow for growth and adaptation. As adults, this means that we can affect our neural pathways and steer them in the direction of secure attachment. We are fundamentally designed to heal. Even if our childhood was less than ideal, our secure attachment system is biologically programmed in us, and our job is to find out more about what's interfering with it and learn what we can do to make those secure tendencies more dominant. Our goal is to excavate our secure attachment so that it will eventually prevail over any relational trauma or attachment disruption that comes up—or at least that we might become more resilient and recover more quickly from distress.

We can never be completely safe, but we can move toward relative safety. We will never have our needs met perfectly, and we will never be (nor have) the perfect parent. Thankfully, that's not required for deep and lasting healing. As we grow out of our wounded self and become a more securely attached, resilient being, we can foster the same process in others, becoming intimacy initiators and connection coaches for our families, friends, and the larger world. When you get right down to it, that's what this book is about.

Let's take a look at both sides of our parents' behavior. Each of us is a work in progress, and I'm sure your parents had some unfinished business along with their more admirable qualities. You may find this exercise helpful in taking a deeper look into what was problematic and painful as well as the gifts your family bestowed. So often our memories of difficult times overshadow the benefits we may have gained, so this exercise is aimed at helping us see more of the whole picture—to acknowledge and grieve wounds as well as celebrate wisdom gained. Of course, often we gain wisdom and compassion from healing our wounds as well.

EXERCISE Perfectly Imperfect

Part One—What Was Missing or Hurtful

You may want to start this exercise by making a list of the shortcomings or failings of each of your parents—those circumstances or behaviors that had the most negative influence on you as a child. *What happened* is significant, and *how* you internalized it is even more so. Sometimes it's easier to recount our parents' negative attributes than it is to remember any of their positive ones, especially for those of us with the ambivalent or disorganized attachment style. Our negative experiences may overshadow the everyday neutral or basically good experiences we may have had until we regain a sense of them after healing many early wounds. People with the avoidant attachment style tend to see their histories as mostly fine until feelings of longing resurface and they realize what they missed relationally.

Part Two—What Was Beneficial or Supportive

My mother was a tough teacher. She lived with unresolved emotional distress, but she was also fun loving and generous. Despite sometimes being a less-than-ideal parent, she had her own ways of expressing her love to me with special celebrations, generous gift-giving, helping me with projects close to my heart, and shopping for fun bargains we called "treasure hunting." My mother also contributed substantially to her community (running telegrams between soldiers and families during WWII, helping with volunteer projects at the hospital, and working with different nonprofit groups). My father was similarly complex: He was out of touch with his emotional self and gone a lot for his work, yet he was able to convey his love quietly in a steadfast way through providing for the family, locking the doors at night, fixing my bike, teaching me to water ski, and grilling great food for picnics. He also had the core value of volunteerism that survives in our family to this day. Both of my parents did the best they could under the circumstances, and together they taught us important core values.

Try looking at each of your parents through the lens of how they may have shown you their love. Write down all the ways you have learned important lessons, skills, and insights from your most important caregivers. It can help to describe your mother and father on their best days. As best you can, give them the benefit of the doubt and consider that they were doing the very best they could with whatever level of unresolved trauma or attachment injury they lived with, as well as with whatever resources, education, and healing strategies they had available to them at that time. See if you can detect their deep care amid their imperfections and harming behaviors, no matter how murky or inarticulate they were in expressing that love for you. What do you find?

MEMORY AND THE ORIGINAL
RELATIONAL BLUEPRINT

It helps to look at how our *original relational blueprint* is built and how that template gets imported into our adult relationships, usually without us even knowing it. Since we're not aware of that process, we act out all sorts of patterns and behaviors without knowing why, often blaming ourself or our partners unfairly. Unresolved trauma can limit our life in ongoing, fundamental ways. Specifically, our unresolved attachment history—the source of our original relational blueprint—can sneak into our adult relationships and cause all kinds of problems. This is unavoidable as long as we are not aware of the source of these destructive patterns. We may repeat these patterns again and again, blind to our own behaviors but able to see the same behaviors unfolding in the lives of those close to us. We act out what we can't see or understand unless the light of awareness and compassion extinguishes the dark places that keep us wounded and unavailable.

So we want to understand how our original relational blueprint forms, how to identify when things are going right, how to foster a safe environment for ourselves, how to know when things aren't going so well, and how to keep from succumbing to definable patterns of disrupted attachment. When we make our original blueprint more conscious, we can actually help ourselves heal and regain healthy attachment patterns that will benefit us for the rest of our lives. Even if we didn't grow up with secure attachment, we can learn it later. To this end, we will engage in practices to gradually stimulate our implicit memory of the blueprints we formed, making them more explicit, thereby allowing us to process them, integrate them, and gain a greater sense of healing and resolution.

Along the way, we'll be enhancing and updating those original, limiting blueprints with some new patterns—options that weren't included the first time around and that are invaluable for greater satisfaction and well-being. Our innate capacity for updating blueprints learned long ago is what brain researchers call "memory reconsolidation,"[10] which Bruce Ecker and colleagues have translated from lab studies into a natural process of personal growth and change. We can't change our factual history, of course, but we can change the rules, roles, meanings, beliefs, and coping tactics we formed based on the original events, in order to let go of some limiting factors that restrain us from the promise of secure attachment. It's not about denying what happened to us; it's about opening to a more expansive capacity, now and in the future.

THE EXERCISES

We'll examine our attachment disruptions and address them through new perspectives and experiential exercises. In this way, we can experience a correction to those disruptions and begin to feel what secure attachment is like. Some of these exercises will feel more beneficial to you than others, and which ones feel the most useful may change over time. These practices might appear simple, but keep in mind that they're meant to tap into or initiate a larger process. They work to open the door just a little at a time so that you can begin to understand and take care of yourself and others a little better.

These experiential exercises can affect you in different ways. Sometimes when we initiate a corrective experience and actually get what we need, we may feel relief and a surge of resiliency that is strengthening. Or we may feel the relief, but it takes us to a deeper awareness of what had been missing in a very painful way. When this happens, we need time and support to grieve that loss before we can take in the resource and repair. Both of these experiences are essential and relevant to healing, so I want to emphasize going at your own pace. The point isn't to throw open the door all at once.

It's important that you allow these positive experiential exercises to influence you—to have a felt-sense experience in your embodied and emotional self. These are the corrective experiences I mentioned earlier, and they're essential to memory reconsolidation, which is the brain's natural, neural process that can produce transformational change: the full, permanent elimination of an acquired behavior or emotional response. Having memories go back into your brain with positive resources encoded in a new way is like planting a positive virus that shifts the memory of the wound in a healing direction toward resolution. You don't necessarily forget what happened or the truth of the original situation, but often you are freer from the discomfort that may have been haunting you.

On the other hand, some exercises can call up old wounds, and that can feel frightening. When you stir the pot, something unpleasant sometimes rises to the top. That's normal. When you access your original relational blueprint and tap into your implicit memory—which is more body-focused and not usually conscious—you will feel as if those old experiences are happening in the moment. It doesn't feel like something that happened years ago; it feels like it's happening to you right now. You may not be aware of yourself as an adult in your living room, for example, and may be drawn back in time to when an unresolved wound occurred and can still be painfully triggered. You may find your awareness limited to an inner child state such that you lose your sense of being an adult and are reexperiencing an event with all the relevant sights, sounds, smells, emotions, and sensations from an earlier time. It doesn't matter how many decades ago that experience was imprinted—you feel it in the moment as if it were happening now, fresh again. Understandably, this can be frightening and confusing. If this occurs during any of the explorations and exercises in this book, remember that this is normal. You can ground yourself somewhat by recalling that you are tapping into an early memory and excavating it and that the results of such brave inquiry can be disorienting.

If something comes up that feels too intense, you can always back off or take a break. Since we're working with early experiences in your implicit memory, it's important to take good care of yourself. Be mindful to not let it become overwhelming. Take a time-out. You can always come back to an exercise at another time. You can also try these practices in the presence of someone safe and supportive—a trained therapist or a loving friend or partner. This can be especially helpful, and it's a wonderful example in itself of self-care.

You can also choose to focus only on building the secure attachment skills (SAS) I talk about at various points in the book. These aren't as likely to trigger a sense of overwhelm, and they're things you can practice and build on to improve the quality of any relationship in your life.

ASSESSMENT QUESTIONS

Each of the next four chapters ends with an informal set of questions. These questions aren't meant to be definitive, exhaustive, or even overly scientific; they're just there to help you assess how much you align with the attachment style discussed in each chapter. My guess is that you'll already have a pretty good idea after reading each chapter whether that type of adaptation is alive in you, but the questions may help spell it out a little better for you. And I hope it goes without saying that these questions aren't intended to box you in, making you fit into one of four predetermined categories. In fact, I hope that going through the chapter-ending questions will help you see just how individualized and fluid your attachment patterning can be, at times depending on the person you are with and focused on.

When you answer the questions at the conclusion of each of these chapters, I suggest you do it twice. Answer first from the perspective of when you are relaxed, and then answer from the perspective of when you feel stressed (under stress, we tend to revert to our original attachment patterning influenced from the deficits of our caretakers in our infant-parent pairs). Notice how the results differ. You can also experiment with answering the questions as they relate to different important relationships you've been in over the years—with parents, partners, and others.

THE PAYOFF

When we learn more about our attachment patterning and examine it with clarity and kindness, we can begin to take things less personally and gain more compassion for ourself and others. We can become familiar with our attachment history through a new—and hopefully softer—lens, understanding more about how certain patterns repeat themselves over the course of our life. When we see that so much of what occurs in our adult relationships goes back to early interactions for which we have no memory, we can then let go of some of the blame we place on ourself and others for the relational woes that inevitably arise. Understanding ourself frees us up to understand others, and that helps us better recognize what they're going through. All of this expedites our healing. And as we heal, we align more with secure attachment, which increases our capacity to love. Our nervous system and brain naturally desire healthy environments and relationships, so when we orient toward secure attachment, we give our brain more adaptive options to choose from. Secure attachment provides us greater access to a variety of brain functions and helps our nervous system become more regulated. Challenges don't throw us as easily as they once did, and we find ourself becoming more and more resilient. We can be with ourself better—becoming more aware of our own thoughts, feelings, and reactions—and we can resonate better with others, which means we become more open and vulnerable to their experiences. Finally, we become more attuned to the relational field between ourself and others—the dynamic created when we come together. Dan Siegel refers to the sense of "MWe"—that is, *me* and *we* together.[11] With secure attachment, we start to want what's good for all of us—what's good for the planet and the entire human community, regardless of community or country or gender or what have you. We begin to tap into the interconnectedness of the whole human family.

There's no denying that this work can be challenging. But consider the payoff: discovering your true self, healing, developing your innate ability to connect with others, increased intimacy, greater authenticity, and a safer vulnerability.

In the next chapter, we'll take an in-depth look at what secure attachment is and what it isn't. There's a lot of confusion out there that I hope to clarify a bit. Understanding what secure attachment is from the beginning will help us reorient ourself in that direction and assist us in building a healthy relationship template. As you'll see, turning toward secure attachment means becoming more aligned with healthy connection and bonding and less affiliated with our own reactivity and pain. It means choosing something more beneficial—for ourself, for our loved ones, and for the world.

1

SECURE ATTACHMENT

Although secure attachment can sound out of reach or like a fantasy goal for many of us, it's how we're fundamentally designed to operate. No matter how unattainable it seems, secure attachment is always there, just waiting to be uncovered, recalled, practiced, and expressed. We might lose access to it from time to time, but we never lose our inherent capacity for secure attachment. Over time, we can also learn to embody secure attachment more naturally so that when we get stressed or triggered by something in our lives, we don't automatically follow the insecurely attached thoughts, feelings, and actions that don't serve us well. As we familiarize ourself more with secure attachment, our relationships become easier and more rewarding—we're less reactive, more receptive, more available for connection, healthier, and much more likely to bring out the securely attached tendencies in others.

So, with all of this good stuff in mind, I want to give you a clear idea of what secure attachment looks like. But first, let's get clear on what secure attachment *isn't*.

My mother used to say, "You have a roof over your head and three meals a day, what are you complaining about?" And some people think that these bare essentials—having a home, food, basic medical care, and so on—are enough. In one way of viewing the world, they're certainly enough, but secure attachment requires a lot more than that.

I needed a lot more than that as a child, as does every child. Secure attachment doesn't mean that we get everything a child could ever want, or that we're spoiled, or that everything always goes right, or that we're never upset by life, or that our parents are absolute saints. And, thankfully, it doesn't mean that we need to be perfect as parents in order to foster secure attachment in our own children.

Ed Tronick is a pioneer in the field of developmental psychology. According to his research, we need to be in attunement with our loved ones just 30% of the time.[1] When you think about it that way, that's a fairly reachable bar. It probably doesn't mean that you can be a terrible parent the other 70% of the time, but I'd say it's a pretty clear message that we can all do our best and relax.

Secure attachment also isn't a type of personality, so I don't want to give you the idea that we're all aiming to be buttoned-down, nice types who take ourself seriously all the time. Nor is secure attachment a type of delusional optimism that isn't connected to the trials and daily problems of the real world. Okay, so if secure attachment doesn't mean just having one's basic needs met, doesn't require a life of ongoing perfection, and doesn't refer to a type of weirdly cheerful and disconnected person, then what is it? In short, secure attachment is attunement. It reflects a positive-enough environment that creates and engenders basic trust.

Here are some markers to spell it out a little better for you:

> **Protection.** Particularly for children, secure attachment means that we feel taken care of and watched over by our parents, who act as our sentinels for safety. They pay attention to what we're doing during the day, know who we're hanging out with, and—depending on our age—make sure that a responsible adult is supervising us when they themselves are not around. That's not something I experienced much of when I was growing up. Times were different, and kids ran free. My parents expected me to be home by six for dinner, but before that particular time, they had little idea of what I was doing, where it was happening, or who I was with. I didn't have playdates and engaged in few after-school activities.

I came home when I was hungry, and my family was mostly clueless about my whereabouts until I told them.

When our parents provide us with a sense of being protected, it primes us to do a better job of taking care of ourself as we mature. Just as with the relationship between interactive regulation and self-regulation, we learn to take care of ourself by receiving appropriate protection early on from the important adults in our lives. As adults, we feel secure with our loved ones and community, in addition to engendering a sense of protection for them, as well.

Presence and Support. For kids, support means that we have compassionate parents who are on our side. They are present in our lives, they have our backs, and they understand and *get* us. That's the wonderful sense of contingency I mentioned earlier. And with a partner or friend, support means that we enjoy this rarefied space of truly knowing one another and feeling known and appreciated in a way that's genuinely nourishing. We feel that we have people we can completely depend on. Securely attached people naturally seek out support when they need it, in addition to freely offering support to others.

Autonomy and Interdependence. As children, we develop autonomy when we receive protection and support from our parents, but not to the degree that they supervise and monitor every little detail of our lives. In other words, parents can do their jobs without going overboard and stifling independence. We can just be kids. When age appropriate, we can go off by ourself for a while, explore the world, and make our own discoveries and mistakes. And when we come back home, we know that our parents are there for us, available to reconnect and love us just as they always have. They give us the loving space in which to mature, without the perils of constant interaction or of habitual screen time with little or no face-to-face, in-person interactions at all. When we develop the capacity for positive dependence and the capacity for independence, we gain the true gift of interdependence—where we can give and receive support and love as well as have our needs expressed and met with true mutuality.

The same holds true for our adult relationships. The autonomous aspect of secure attachment means that we can transition fluidly between alone time and together time without it being a big deal. The balance and flow between being together and being apart is just right. Note that I'm not presenting autonomy as synonymous with *isolation* or an over-developed sense of *self-reliance*.

Relaxation. Relationships in which we can let our guard down, relax, and be ourself are invaluable. We can joke with each other, feel spontaneous, and laugh together. Young children absolutely love it when you play with them, enter their world, and have fun together. When the container of a relationship is safe and supportive, all of this can happen naturally, which means that our relationships are characterized by fun and play, lightness and humor. To put it another way: we delight in one another's company, and we look forward to being together because it's just so enjoyable. But this relaxation isn't without boundaries, especially for children. It exists in tandem with age-appropriate limitations and consequences. It's important that kids know that boundaries and closeness can go hand in hand.

Trust. Trust is an important topic that is often misunderstood. Most of us have learned to trust certain things about people through our experiences of them. For example, if Jack is always on time, I quickly begin to trust that he will be punctual when I make plans with him. I've learned that Amara always pays me back, Brandon is always there for me in a pinch, and Tyra is a wonderful partner to go on adventures with. I've learned to rely on them for each of these attributes, and that's a nice, practical kind of trust—but that's not the kind of trust I'm talking about here.

The trust I'm talking about is a sense that the world is a predominantly good place—a conviction that even in the darkest of times, healing, understanding, and goodness will prevail. This kind of trust typically comes from a positive childhood environment, where we were held and raised most of the time with "good enough parenting," to use a phrase coined by English pediatrician and psychoanalyst Don Winnicott, which means a positive "holding environment" that engenders basic trust.[2] With this quality of caregiving, we grow up believing that other people are fundamentally good and well-meaning, and we trust that basic fact in our interactions with others.

People who grow up with significant relational wounds, however, often have a confused relationship with trust. Either they don't trust anyone whatsoever as a blanket policy—distrusting any situation, government, community, personal relationship, and so on—or they have little discrimination at all and blindly trust any and all situations and people who come their way. I call this latter tendency *throwing trust indiscriminately*, and it's a recipe for disaster. These people regularly get into edgy or dangerous relationships that would set off red flags for other people, and by doing so, they set themselves up to get wounded even further. But when I talk about trust, I'm not talking about something naïve and dangerous, but something fundamentally healing and restorative. It's a bedrock trust in the basic goodness of life—a fundamental positivity toward what life is all about—but with a ton of healthy discernment. This type of trust empowers and allows for authentic forgiveness. Healing our fundamental sense of trust is a large part of our journey to restoring ourself in secure attachment.

Resilience. It makes a world of difference whether we consider the universe to be malevolent or friendly. How we envision the world directly influences the way we experience it. When we enjoy a basic trust in the world, it means that we're intrinsically more optimistic and unflappable. We recover from hardships more quickly, and we're able to pull our resources together quite well when trouble eventually hits the proverbial fan. We're better able to access support, ask for assistance, and help ourself find solutions. In doing so, we learn to trust the world and ourself even more.

GATHERING SUPPORT

Now that you know a little more about what secure attachment looks like, I invite you to apply this knowledge as a relational resource. The following exercise involves reviewing your relationships a lot like you did in the exercises in the introduction.

EXERCISE   Summoning Secure Attachment

Begin by sitting in a chair and bringing your awareness to your body. Take a moment to feel your feet on the floor and notice your breathing. When you're somewhat grounded, mentally scan the important relationships in your life. Mostly, I want you to look for those people who stand out as representatives of secure attachment. Certain aspects of these people, their behavior, or your interactions with them give you a sense of trust, safety, support, reliability, connection, understanding, and presence. Just notice who shows up. It could be anyone in your past or present—family members, pets, teachers, coaches, therapists, friends, or even strangers.

Gather these people around you. Visualize yourself being surrounded by them in a protective, caring space. What happens with you emotionally when you do this? Do you find yourself becoming more tender, or perhaps more protected and guarded? Do you feel more open or closed than you did before? Where do you feel sensation in your body? Pay attention to what it's like to be with these people. Sense their goodwill and note all the physical and emotional details of this experience.

FOSTERING SECURE ATTACHMENT IN YOURSELF AND OTHERS

After all this talk about what secure attachment looks like, it's not unusual for people to give themselves a hard time. It seems like such a high bar, and when we look at it that way, it's easy to feel not quite up to snuff. I can relate to that feeling, and I think it's quite normal for everyone to feel that way from time to time.

We all have emotional reactions we're not proud of, and most of us contribute our fair share to arguments and unnecessarily difficult conversations. And many of us simply aren't as present as we'd like to be. We don't feel quite *here* enough—either we're distracted by one thing or another, or we're not as attentive as we think we should be. Again, all of this is normal. Most of these things happen regularly—at least they do for me! The main point is to care enough to notice when things are less than ideal. That means having enough presence to know that things are a little off and enough compassion to want to do a retake, to make things better. There's more wiggle room than you'd think. Remember Ed Tronick's research that I mentioned earlier indicating that being in attunement with our loved ones only 30% of the time could still foster secure attachment?[3] It's okay to goof up, make mistakes, and be less than our perfect self. The attachment system is a forgiving system, and it makes a world of difference to register when we miss each other and mend when things go awry as soon as possible.

We can all do a better job, of course, and that's where practice comes in. So for the rest of this chapter, I want to offer you ways to practice fostering secure attachment in yourself and others. These are methods for boosting your secure attachment skills (SAS). The idea isn't to ace every one of these, but pick out a couple that you feel called to work on and practice these the best you can. Hopefully, there's SAS here for everyone—skills you can offer others in your life, skills to practice mutually in your relationships, and skills to encourage secure attachment in yourself.

SAS #1   Listen Deeply

Let's start with one of the more obvious skills. We all know the value of listening, but most of us haven't actually taken the time to develop our listening skills in any ongoing way. When we listen deeply, reflect back to the other person, and ask questions that help us understand them, we allow the other person to inform us of what's going on with them—not in a superficial way, but in a manner that empowers them to really dive in, feel their feelings, and express them to us until we truly get them. By listening in this way, we can provide that sense of contingency I spoke of earlier. We're not simply listening until they take a breath so that we can jump into the conversation and say what's on our mind. Listening deeply means that we respond with considerate questions meant to foster and convey understanding, and we always give space before explaining our perspective.

It's important to note that when we listen to another person, we don't have to believe or agree with what they are saying. They could be talking about anything—accusing us of flirting with someone else at a restaurant, or abandoning them at a Christmas party, or forgetting to follow up with something around the house that we promised to do (washing the dishes, for example). Really listening to someone means that we don't immediately respond to what they're saying with denial or criticism. Instead of negating their concern or getting into an argument about it, we just listen. That's it. And we can open up the contingency space even further by trying to resonate with them. "I understand why you'd be upset about that, and I can see that really hurt you," for example. In other words, listening in this way means you're offering to hold—to contain—whatever it is that they're dealing with and be present with them, regardless of their emotional responses and reactions.

I am continually surprised by the power of listening in my own life. I was teaching in Europe a few years ago, and there were some participants who were unhappy about the way we were running the training. When they brought it up, I did my best to listen and invite any and all to speak about their concerns. As a leader, I think this is extremely important to do. I tried to keep the conversation going until everyone who wanted to say something was able to give voice to their unhappiness, and the process took close to an hour. I tried not to be involved other than just opening the space for their feelings to surface and be heard. When they had finished speaking, I did my best to recap what I had heard, asked for clarification, and invited them all to take a cappuccino and cookie break while my staff and I met to address the issues that had been brought up.

During our meeting, my team and I took to heart what we'd heard and came up with some direct ways to better support the group. I told the participants what we planned to do for them—taking into account as many requests as possible—and then we moved back into the training itself. Interestingly, when we received the feedback forms after the training was completed, this particular exchange was the thing people appreciated most. They valued having a facilitator and team who would actually listen to them and take the time to address their issues instead of brushing them aside or shutting them down when difficult topics arose. This took place in a culture that is a bit authoritarian, so it made a substantial difference for this group to have leaders who responded openly and without harshness, misuse of power, or criticism. This was an incredibly important lesson for me.

I think most of us have this in common: more than we want to be convinced otherwise or placated, we just really want to be heard on a deep level. That can be hard at times, of course, because relationships can bring up a lot of stuff for us, and it's natural to have challenges when dealing with other people, especially those closest to us. But if we can do our best to listen, we can make the best of difficult situations, and we'll have a much better chance of closing the gap between us and the person we're listening to.

SAS #2   Practice Presence

Listening is one of the ways we can show presence, which is one of the most important gifts we can give ourself and others in relationships. Presence isn't a static thing; it's a way of being. Presence means showing up, paying attention, and letting the other person know that we're there for them with whatever's going on. It means we do our best to put aside our own worries and concerns and be with them in an undistracted way. This can be hard in today's world when it's common to be on our devices so much of the time, but I highly recommend setting your phone or tablet aside when you want to show someone else that you're truly present for them. Of course, this is impossible to do perfectly all the time, but there are certain things we can do to practice presence in order to become more available to others, as well as to ourself.

I have an acquaintance named Jim who is a busy therapist and coach. He has lots of demands on his time, but he told me that when he goes back home to visit his parents, he tries to leave all his business behind. He doesn't take calls; he doesn't go on the Internet; he doesn't do anything that might distract him from being fully present with his mother and father. Jim does his best to devote those three or four days to them, full-time. He reports that it has utterly transformed their relationship and enabled them to heal quite a bit just from Jim showing up like that.

So I decided to give it a try myself. Before, when I'd go visit my parents, I'd try to catch up on work and get to all the calls and emails I hadn't answered yet. I stopped doing that when I was with them, pledging to be 100% there in a way I hadn't before. I gave my mother pedicures and manicures and watched TV with her, and we enjoyed some valuable and interesting discussions about what was important to her in life, what had meaning, what she regretted, what was funny, and many other topics, including history and fashion. I went on bike rides with my dad and hung out with him in his workshop fixing things—well, he did most of the fixing, but I was there as a companion. I even brought a camera and made a movie, interviewing my parents about their lives. They talked about their siblings, friends, teachers, and parents; their first jobs, first loves, and first kisses; high school dances and the prom. My dad gave me a little more embarrassing info than I had counted on as he explained his early dating rituals behind the ice cream shop where he worked after school. He shared about not being allowed to dance or have parties as a boy due to his strict religious upbringing, and my mom relayed a surprising story about visiting a morgue on prom night on a dare. They both described hanging around the radio as a family and enjoying the early TV programming in the 1950s. In short, I learned a lot of delightful things about them, and being present in this way changed our relationship. We were even able to get some closure on stuff left hanging in our relationship from my childhood. In turn, this opened up the space for more intimacy and connection.

Committing to remain undistracted with another person in a world that is so full of distractions is a powerful and fulfilling practice. For most of us today, this requires putting our screens and devices to the side and not letting them distract and divide us, at least for a while. Try it at dinner sometime: put everyone's silenced cell phone in a basket while you're enjoying the meal together and see what a difference it makes in your ability to connect. Attention is an extremely valuable commodity, and I recommend as much device-free, face-to-face time as you can manage.

People know if you're fully present or not, and it matters to them. Try being present when you're on the phone sometime. Instead of doing something else—like surfing the Internet or washing the dishes—sit down and try to be as present and attentive as you possibly can. Give undistracted time to the people who are important to you and watch how that transforms your relationships. If you want to find out more about the power of presence in relationships, I strongly recommend reading *Year of Yes* by Shonda Rhimes. Counselor, researcher, and author Kim John Payne has written a lot on this topic, too.

SAS #3 Attune

Attunement is almost a synonym for empathy or secure attachment itself. I'd like to offer it here as a skill we can hone that involves a wonderful combination of listening, presence, and a lot of compassion. Psychologist and author Dan Goleman credits Paul Ekman, a therapist and pioneer in the study of emotions and their relationship to facial expressions, for outlining three types of empathy: cognitive, emotional, and compassionate (something that Dan calls *empathic concern*).[4] Cognitive empathy refers to our ability to get someone else's take on the world, whereas emotional empathy means that we resonate with their feelings. Empathic concern is true attunement: it means that we get all of the above, but we're also in there with the other person in a way that lets them know they aren't alone. We're personally touched by their joys, and when they're struggling, we want to do something about it; we want to take action to help.

So attunement means a lot of things. It means becoming curious about another person's experience and working to understand what they're all about, discovering them in new ways and trying to resonate with them. How do they see the world? How do they experience their own feelings? And whatever emotions or situations arise, attunement also means that we do our best to connect with other people and let them know we're there. Attunement is what enables that sense of contingency to arise. It lets the other person know that we really get them—that we're by their side. This is an invaluable experience to receive and to offer another person.

Being dedicated to attunement also keeps us in touch with when we fall out of attunement with others, which is crucial knowledge to have in relationships. We're oriented toward connection, but we're also aware when that connection isn't quite as we'd like it to be. If you feel you are not quite in sync with someone or are concerned that you don't fully understand their situation or their feelings, ask the person to tell you more about what they are trying to share. Ask caring and clarifying questions.

SAS #4   Engage in Joint Attention

The skills that follow—the SAS that are intended for people to practice together—can be seen as a subset of joint attention. Joint attention means mutually being there for each other, no matter what you're doing: meditating together, dancing to your favorite song, telling jokes, making meals, or exercising. Any activity can serve to foster more secure attachment with your partner, child, family member, or friend when enacted with joint attention. You could be watching a movie on the flat-screen from your couch and still practice joint attention (for example, occasionally making eye contact with each other, laughing together, or having a conversation later about the film).

SAS #5   Maintain Contact

One of the hallmarks of secure attachment is consistent responsiveness. Contact maintenance means that you do your best to keep connected to the other person, whether through eye contact, touch, texts, or dates to your favorite restaurant. To practice this skill, all it takes is being a little bit more mindful when responding to messages from the other person. Remember that babies cry to express different needs. As adults, we can use words to reach out to others, but sometimes we're not so direct and can employ complaints, arguments, and conflict to gain the connection we're seeking underneath it all. For example, beneath the complaint, "I can't believe you're going off on another business trip without me," is the message, "I really love you, and I want to be with you, and I miss you when you're gone." So keep this in mind in your own relationships. When someone asks you for something, remember that a lot more might be going on than meets the eye. Try to remember that the quality of your response might mean everything to them.

In this regard, timing is important. If a baby calls out, and you wait until the end of the day to respond to that signal cry, chances are that their need will have not been met because they cannot do it themselves yet, and they will be in dire distress. Additionally, they may have a mess of other needs to attend to. If I ask you for something as an adult, and I don't hear back from you for three weeks, it's going to feel like you're not very interested in being connected with me. Even if the answer is no, the response time itself is important. So we need to respond in a timely fashion—with a certain promptness—and the quality of the response should match what the person is asking for, meeting their need as best you can.

Finally, when you're practicing contact maintenance with someone else, it's crucial to avoid keeping score on who is responding the best or the quickest. It should also go without saying that reacting negatively when someone expresses a need doesn't encourage contact maintenance or secure attachment. Of course, we are not always able to respond immediately to our partner's signal cry or request, but we can all improve on answering calls for connection a little more compassionately and promptly.

SAS #6   Be Mindful of Comings and Goings

Like "SAS #4: Engage in Joint Attention," this skill can cover quite a lot of ground. Our attachment systems are sensitive to when people approach us, when they leave, and what happens in our relationships as a result of those transitions. For some of us, meeting up again is more difficult than a departure, and vice versa. It's interesting to pay attention to what happens when people come and go in our daily life. What kind of person are you? Are you sensitive to others approaching you? Do you avoid approaching others yourself? Do you feel distressed when folks say goodbye and leave?

Stan Tatkin recommends a beautiful activity called the "Welcome Home Exercise"[5.] Maybe you're at home making dinner, and your partner comes home from a long day at work. To do this exercise, all you have to do is turn the heat down on the food, walk over to your partner, and give them a big hug. You stay in that full-body, belly-to-belly embrace long enough for both of your bodies to relax and regulate. As I mentioned earlier, our nervous system is built to co-regulate, and this is a way to directly interact with another person's nervous system. You connect your two bodies and regulate each other, which sets the tone for your time together going forward. As it turns out, when you experience another person as neurologically regulating, your body really wants to be with them. Imagine that!

The end of the day when we fall asleep is an important transition for couples. How do you go to bed at night? Couples don't always fall asleep together these days due to work schedules or other commitments, so when you can, it's beneficial to schedule a mindful time during which you say good night to each other. Or if you do fall asleep together, use a ritual to mutually end the day, even if it's just talking about what happened at work for fifteen minutes or so.

One of my favorite couples, Dee and Freddy, have a chocolate lover's ritual that I find brilliant. They each leave a newly discovered chocolate or gourmet truffle on the other's pillow at night so that they can delight in their favorite treat together while debriefing and sharing their day. They routinely take this time to clear and repair anything even slightly disturbing that might have happened during the day between them as well. It's not just a pleasant ritual to end the day with; it's a wonderful gesture of appreciation, connection, and love.

We can do little things like this to begin the day, too. Some people always have breakfast together or make each other coffee or take a walk around the neighborhood. Whatever it is, try to establish a ritual for each other that appreciates the importance of comings and goings. Making this a priority will strengthen your attachment bond.

SAS #7 Use Your Eyes

We're neurologically designed to communicate face-to-face. Texting with words and emojis, responding to each other on social media, and keeping in regular contact through emails all have their place in today's world, but none of these offers the type of fundamental nourishment that comes with physical presence and eye contact. In my work, we often refer to the *attachment gaze* or the *beam gleam* (coined by Patti Elledge, who teaches our DARe workshops). This means using eye contact to impart a feeling of kindness and receptivity to others, or receiving the same from them, or both at the same time. It's that look that says, "You're special to me," or "You're amazing," or "I love you." Think about how your eyes appear to the other person when you look at them. What are you conveying? At some point or another, all of us have received harsh looks from others—shameful, angry, or hateful looks—and getting one of those can shut down your whole being. But the opposite is also true. Just notice what happens when you allow your eyes to express connection and appreciation toward someone else.

Keep in mind, however, that people can avert their gaze when they're experiencing something difficult (shame, for example). It isn't always the best idea to try to maintain or even invite eye contact. Teenagers often find it intrusive or aggressive, and a parent's demand to "look at me when I'm talking to you" usually just invites more estrangement. Sometimes it's better to walk and talk side by side or to take part in predominantly silent activities together, such as fishing, gardening, or sewing. In some cultures, friendly eye contact is interpreted as a sexual invitation; in others, it's a sign of disrespect if children look directly at an adult.

Eye contact isn't always helpful or appropriate, but when it is, it's one of the easiest ways out there to nourish secure attachment. It doesn't cost anything, takes minimal effort, and you can do it at almost any time with very beneficial results in terms of nourishing the attachment bond. Try it when you're at a party with your significant other: shoot them a beam gleam from across the room. Use your eyes to let your loved one know you think they're great, that you appreciate them. It takes maybe two seconds of your time, but I promise it will mean the world to them. You can even practice the attachment gaze with your pets. See how they respond. We'll try this exercise in a different way when we look into avoidant attachment in chapter two.

SAS #8   Play

This is a delightful way to nourish your attachment system. Just think about how much children like to play with each other, imaginary beings, their parents, and other friendly adults. It seems like there's nothing in the world more important to them than playing. As adults, it's easy to become entirely work-focused and to ignore how important play is, but play is a wonderful way to foster connection and trust. We set so many goals in our life, but what if we made fun our priority—actually having fun together? Try a new game with your partner or reintroduce an activity you both enjoyed as children. The object isn't to win, of course, but for you and your partner to enjoy yourselves together.

Increasing playtime is one of the most enjoyable ways to embellish your experience of secure attachment. Get creative and have fun! One of my friends, Sharon, bought her husband a fedora and rented *Casablanca* (his favorite movie). Annie came up with an evening at the batting cages with her husband, even though she had never swung a bat before. Ralph bought tickets to the theater, concerts, and comedy clubs and signed up for cooking classes with his partner. Matt and Suzie took tango lessons together. Miniature golf, hiking, board games, hunting, bird-watching, river rafting, university lectures, wine tasting—the possibilities are endless!

SAS #9   Un-automate

To become more efficient at doing things in the world, the brain does its best to automate processes. For example, after we first learn to ride a bike, we automate the process so that we can repeat it with increasing ease. In the same way, we learn to write, read, add and subtract, and so on. We then automate so that these activities are more efficient; we don't have to think about every step each and every time we do them. Stan Tatkin points out that, unfortunately, we have a tendency to automate our partners.[6] We expect them to behave and respond in a given bandwidth that isn't very flexible, and we can mistakenly believe that we know everything there is to know about this other person, which is ridiculous. Every person in our life is a unique, unfolding universe. It's far more rewarding to attend to this fact and engage them in ways befitting their ongoing miraculousness.

One way to do so is to find new and unusual things to do together. This will help you stay interested and connected to different aspects of those you're close to. Novelty creates attraction in the brain. It keeps our relationships alive, exciting, and passionate. The more we allow for novelty and complexity, the more possibilities we encourage to arise in our relationship, which keeps us interested. So it's important to keep yourself open to all the different possibilities of what your partner could be and who they are and not assume that you already know them, and it's all done. It's not done; it never ends. Every day is a new beginning.

SAS #10   Repair, Repair, Repair

Psychological researcher and clinician John Gottman conducted a study with newlyweds that followed them for six years. The couples who stayed married practiced repairing ruptures in their relationship 86% of the time, whereas those who divorced turned toward each other to repair only 33% of the time.[7] That's a substantial difference. If there's one thing I'd like you to take away from this section, it's the importance of repair.

None of us is present or attuned or playful or all that good at listening all of the time. That's just how it goes. We all make mistakes or aren't up to snuff here and there, and that's where repair comes in. Learning this skill is an essential component to maintaining secure attachment. The challenge is that most of us never learned how to apologize or repair from our original families. As easy as it sounds, I've found it to be rare that we know how to do this, so keep in mind that repair might not be something that comes naturally to you or your partner.

When things go awry, it doesn't really matter who repairs first or who apologizes. Ideally, both people make the repair in a relatively timely way. Of course, sometimes we need to take a time-out to collect ourself. I know I do. But then we come back together so that we can move through whatever disappointment or hurt came up. And it's crucial to recognize when others are trying to repair with us.

If you've ever come home after work and your dog has gotten into the trash or dumped something on the kitchen floor, you know that even animals can display shame when they've done something wrong. My dog Max would approach me with his furry little head down, tentatively wagging his tail, after a heist of the kitchen garbage can. This is a natural response in all of us, and it's important to recognize it in others so that we can regain a sense of contact and togetherness. Dogs are incredibly social animals. If you punish them by putting them out in the yard for twenty minutes, for example, that's about as long as they can take it. Anything more than that will cause them hurt, as if they were outcast or abandoned. Now think about how much more sensitive your children are. Time-outs can be helpful, but they can backfire or cause too much pain if they go on too long. It's far better to stay in contact more and work through a repair. If a child approaches you and says they're sorry or hands you a picture they drew just for you, it's crucial that you learn how to respond open-heartedly to that.

Sometimes when people try to repair with us, we block their attempts. Maybe they didn't apologize just right, were inarticulate, or we don't feel they truly understand how they hurt us, or they made up to us a lot later than we wanted them to. Well, what I'm suggesting is that we all try to be a little more generous. When someone comes forward with some gesture of reconciliation, try to recognize that and appreciate it for what it is as opposed to how it falls short. The benefit of the doubt will benefit both of you.

Of course, we also need to learn how to initiate repair. This involves the listening skill I talked about earlier. Just drop all the explanations, rationalizations, and disagreements and simply listen. Remember that most of what triggers us comes from our attachment history, so when your partner experiences some type of hurt in the relationship, you're usually not dealing with a fresh wound that's only about something you did or didn't do. In other words, you're not likely to set things right by explaining yourself well. There's something deeper going on.

It's okay to make mistakes in relationships. Really, it is. The good news is that these disconnections can make your relationship stronger, as long as you learn how to repair. Ed Tronick reminds us that arriving at a beneficial place in your relationship doesn't happen in a linear, direct way. It's more like sailing, where the wind blows you a little off course, so you make the necessary adjustments. Then the wind blows you the other way, and you make more adjustments back in the direction you want to go, moving in a zigzag fashion toward your desired destination. When you make mistakes in a relationship, the little detours don't have to derail the whole enterprise. Repairing misattunements can build relationship resiliency.[8] Of course, we don't want to cause disconnection on purpose: we mess up enough just by being human. The important thing is to do what we can to find attunement when disconnections inevitably arise.

Are there people in your life who have tried to make repairs with you lately? Take a moment to think about it. Call to mind anyone who has attempted to reach out and connect with you who you've somehow ignored or given the cold shoulder. Maybe you didn't return their most recent text, or you've been delaying your response to a phone message because you don't feel like seeing them in person. What would it be like to open yourself to their repair attempt? Are you willing to try it?

I also want to invite you to think about people you yourself would like to reach out to and repair with. Maybe something feels a little off in your relationship, and you'd like to open up the space to connect again. You might need to own up to your side of a disagreement or maybe apologize for a small hurt of some kind. What would it look like to repair with this person? How might things change in your relationship as a result?

Check this out in your life. Notice what happens when you accept or initiate repair. Sometimes we might offer to repair with someone who is not open to that or who isn't particularly responsive. That's okay, too. Repair is a vital skill to learn and practice regardless of the outcome, and the more we make these efforts, the better we get at them. It's also a way to directly update our relationships. We download the latest software, so to speak, and ideally things start to run a little better. We're able to move forward and increase our relational capacity overall.

In day-to-day relationships, it's helpful to discuss how you might support repair attempts before you're in a space in which one or both of you feels triggered. I think of this as designing a repair ritual. It could be as simple as using a particular word to signal that you're ready for repair. It doesn't have to make sense to anyone else; you could say "watermelon" or "pancakes" or "let's go sailing," especially if the word or phrase is something you both enjoy eating or doing together. Doing this signals that you're ready to reconcile, and that gesture will shift the energy of the argument or bridge the distance that's been created. You could also use a gesture or visual signal, like lighting a candle when you feel ready to apologize. It's a way of saying, "I want to move past this. I really want to reconcile and come back together with you." Maybe the other person also has a candle that says, "Okay, I'm ready to listen and connect with you now."

When I was married to my very tall husband, I would stand on the first step of the staircase when we hugged. So this became our repair ritual: when I was ready, I would go stand on that step, he would recognize it as the signal, and he would come over so that we could hug and reconcile. There are many ways to bring rituals like this into your relationship. It doesn't matter what it looks like as long as it helps you repair, recover, and build resiliency.

SAS #11   Build and Expand Your Resources

I want to turn now to some practices you can do for yourself, by yourself, to promote secure attachment. In the introduction, I mentioned that attachment patterning is not something that happens only in one lifetime—that is, from only the experiences you have in your own childhood. Our attachment style—the plusses and the minuses—can actually be transmitted across generations; in a sense, we inherit the attachment patterning of all our ancestors. For some of us, this might seem like terrible news, but keep in mind that neuroplasticity is part of the design of our nervous system. So while it's true that far too many of us were raised by parents who carried old wounds of their own childhood and the suffering of their ancestors—wounds that never quite healed and caused our parents (and theirs) to struggle their entire lives—it's also true that our attachment adaptations are not written in stone. Some of us are dealing with traumatic legacies, so I'd like to offer some practices that take advantage of our innate neuroplasticity.

Whether conscious or not, some parents who live with ongoing hurt encourage their own children to take care of them. This type of relationship, of course, is the polar opposite of what is supposed to happen. Your parents are supposed to be there to protect you, to meet your needs, and to take care of you—not the other way around. It's not that kids are never supposed to do anything for their parents, but children are not designed or mature enough to solve the problems of adults or operate as a surrogate caregiver or partner. When parents treat their children this way, it often results in some form of insecure attachment. If any of this sounds familiar to you, I invite you to try the following exercises to help reorient you toward secure attachment.

EXERCISE Reversing Role Reversal (with Your Mother/Mother Figure)

Let's begin by imagining your mother. Picture her in front of you as she was growing up. Try to get a clear feeling of who your mother was and what she was all about—what her concerns were, what her needs were, what challenges she faced, and so on. Do your best to sense into her experience as vividly as you can.

Now imagine that your mother had all the support she needed from other caring adults when she faced any hardships. In this fantasy, imagine that she had access to whatever strength, trait, bit of wisdom, or community to help her in exactly the way she needed through her childhood and into adulthood. It's crucial that you don't imagine yourself fulfilling these needs. When you are visualizing in this exercise, imagine that other capable and caring adults were there for her. See your mother surrounded by competent, loving adults who gave her whatever support she required. As your mother's child, you don't need to do anything; you're simply watching it all happen. Observe this movie you are crafting in your imagination. Witness these competent, nourishing adults take care of your mother and notice the details of the results of their care.

Maybe your mother smiles more or walks a little lighter in the world. She's happier, stronger, and more resourced to meet the challenges ahead. Notice the changes in her as she gets what she needs. She may be growing, healing, having fun, and enjoying more energy. She may be able to be more attentive and less resentful as a parent.

One of my clients, Lisa, imagined her mother having friends like Mary Tyler Moore's character on the TV show of the same name from the 1970s. Lisa imagined her mother in a book club full of these kinds of independent, professional women in contrast to her actual mother, who felt overwhelmed and shut down having ten children, one after another, and being totally dependent on her husband. As Lisa's imaginary, freer mom enjoyed the company of strong, interdependent women, Lisa's own feelings of guilt and shame for being a burden to her mother lifted, and she felt freer as well. She no longer felt she had to sacrifice herself to care for her mother since her mother now (in her mind) had her book club friends and could be supported by other adults. Even though the book club was imaginary, this scene allowed Lisa to disentangle herself.

Now turn your attention to yourself. How do you feel as a child with your mother now that you imagine her as completely taken care of, protected, supported, enjoyed, and satisfied? What do you notice in your body? What's happening with you emotionally? What's the difference in your experience now that she has competent adults in her life and does not need you or any other child to take care of her? Explore these questions and experience any new thoughts, feelings, and sensations that come up for you.

Take a moment to write down what this practice was like for you. What happens when you imagine that your mother was well resourced? Many people experience a profound sense of relief after engaging in this exercise. Some are able to visualize enjoying their childhood; they may feel carefree for the first time ever. My friend Alan did this exercise and saw his previously exhausted mother now cooking in the kitchen, humming a tune, and smiling. Then he saw his father come into the room, wrap his arms around his mother's waist, and nuzzle her as they

swayed in the kitchen, dancing, while she occasionally stirred t
This picture was quite different from what actually happene
childhood. His alcoholic father was prone to anger, and his
was frightened of him. Regardless, Alan allowed himself to see the
picture of something different, and in so doing, he noticed changes
in himself. When he envisioned his parents as connected and loving,
his imagined family environment was supportive, harmonious, and
joyful. Since he wasn't feeling like he had to rush off to take care of his
mother in some way, he began to feel calmer, more carefree, and less
anxious as a child. Alan felt he could focus more easily in play with his
siblings and on projects he loved, like building model airplanes. Going
through the back door via this powerful imaginary process, my friend
gained a glimpse of what secure attachment can feel like. This is not a
minor thing. It's highly important that the emotional, psychological,
and spiritual parts of you get a chance to feel how different secure
attachment can be and to embody those new feelings. This gives your
secure attachment a chance to say "hello," and you get a glimpse of
what secure attachment actually feels like so that you can begin to
reorient toward it today as an adult.

EXERCISE   Reversing Role Reversal
(with Your Father/Father Figure)

Now let's try the same exercise with your father. Do your best to tap
into your father's experience. Underneath everything, what is it that your
father needs? What might his core wound be as you perceive him more
precisely? Try to see him as thoroughly and clearly as you can—his
challenges, deficits, wounds, and gifts. Imagine that some wise elders,
compassionate friends, or caring family members are there for him.
If you could invent the perfect guide for him, who would it be? Again,
this guide, mentor, or elder is someone other than yourself—an adult
who is competent, kind, and dependable and knows just what to do
or suggest. See this person (or persons) supporting your father through
difficult times, raising him with gentleness and humor, or simply being
there for him through whatever he needs. Watch how your father responds.

See him smile and grow up strong and resourced as he feels supported as an adult, as well. Imagine what the changes look like as he moves through life supported and loved in this way.

Now turn your focus toward yourself. What are you feeling right now? What's happening in your heart? What sensations arise in your body? What's it like to see your father so well resourced, supported, and loved? What's different in your experience now that you see him taken care of? With his needs met, your father may have more energy and capacity to be a better parent to you and your siblings. What happens when his capacities are freed up to be available for you as the child? What shifts for you?

All of us are born full of love and compassion, and as we grow up, we're quite aware of the suffering around us, especially the suffering of our parents. Naturally, we want to fill the holes in their lives, heal their wounds, and meet their unmet needs. But we can't. First, it isn't our job to do. Second, we're not old enough or resourced enough to pull it off even if we try. So if we grow up with parents who need us to take care of them somehow, we go forward in life always feeling like we let them down—we're not quite enough, or we're always failing to one degree or another.

I suggest you go through this practice several times. Try it with other mother figures and father figures, but focus on just one relationship at a time; it works better if you're visualizing a single person rather than a group. Even though this experience is imaginary, it will help to heal relational wounds. It doesn't matter how different your actual history is from the imagined version. As you bring up memories and infuse them with positive counterpoints, it doesn't change the past, but it does mix the original event in with up-to-date resources.

With memory reconsolidation, when we contact the memory of the original wound, it becomes vulnerable to change. When we have a felt-sense experience of secure attachment, for example, that new resource may become part of the original memory. And when the brain is confronted by the old injury alongside the relevant corrective experience—such as the new memory with new resources—the brain is designed to choose the more adaptive scenario or response. Planting a seed of experience around secure attachment gives the brain an opportunity to shift in a healthier direction. So, to be clear, this exercise is not about negating history; it's about moving forward into a brighter, empowered future.

When we've grown up with parents who harmed us or otherwise didn't meet our needs, it can sometimes be difficult to help them as they age and need more assistance. If we can heal our history, we may be able to be more available to our parents in an authentic way as they reach the end of their life. We may see their unresolved attachment wounds surface again more profoundly under the stress of increasing vulnerabilities as they age—for example, excessive clinginess or unrealistic self-sufficiency. In the latter, a parent may get angry when they have to ask for help from you or others due to frailty. My friend's mother Edith became distrustful and a bit paranoid that her kids were taking advantage of her financially when they set up a trust for her—nothing was further from the truth. Her loss of financial autonomy was disturbing to her as her children paid her bills and filed her taxes for her. If attachment injuries resurface or continue for your parents as they age—which is common—you may be called on to practice your secure attachment skills to support them in this stage of life as well.

SAS #12 Attend to the Good

When we're recovering from trauma, it's important that we examine our wounds, gently tend to them, and compassionately help ourself recover. But we need to be mindful not to fall into what author and healer Caroline Myss calls "woundology"—that is, defining our lives solely by our wounds and struggles.[9] Doing so can prevent us from growing and changing how we experience the world and our relationships. For this reason, it's equally important to nourish the positive in our life, and that's what learning SAS is all about. We want to develop the ability to recognize what's going right in our life and find ways to foster our relationship to happiness and well-being.

Just as plants grow toward the sun, we flower when we orient ourself toward secure attachment. To this end, it's valuable to recognize the good feelings that go along with secure attachment. Most of us are already quite talented at recognizing hurt feelings when things go wrong, but we need to develop a type of radar to know when things are going right. How well do we pick up the cues for true connection? How good are we at orienting ourself toward the "zoetropic zone"? In Greek, *zoe* means "life," and *trope* means "turn" or "toward," so *zoetropic* means "turning toward life," and the zoetropic zone is characterized by life-affirming feelings and experiences—like a sunflower naturally turning toward the light as it grows. That's what we're after here. Essentially, we want to be familiar with what works for and benefits us—that's what we want to highlight in our lives. I hope it goes without saying that I'm not talking about simply ignoring our traumas and wounds. That's obviously not helpful. But the approach I'm recommending here goes beyond focusing *only* on our struggles.

I mentioned Rick Hanson in the introduction. This topic is his specialty, and I highly recommend his work (check out his books *Hardwiring Happiness*, *Buddha's Brain*, *Just One Thing*, or anything else of his that you can find). Most relevant to the SAS we're talking about here, Rick emphasizes just how important it is to connect with positive experiences long enough to actually alter old neural pathways. Remember that the brain is quite capable of doing this; in fact, it's designed to heal and grow in a positive way. For this reason, it's important to open ourself to the corrective experiences provided by practices like the ones above. Paying attention to positive imagery and infusing memories with resources will enhance our connection to secure attachment, and this creates the change we want in our life.

I also recommend emphasizing positive media, books, and experiences for you and your family. You can provide your secure attachment system with lots of nourishment by watching prosocial TV programs and movies, as well as reading affirming books or attending positive workshops. I recommend television not because I want to get you hooked on any bad habits, but to offer something readily available if you are going to watch TV anyway. Personally, I really enjoyed watching *Parenthood*—a show on NBC about the Braverman family.

Even though they experience a lot of conflicts and go through various difficult experiences, this family finds a way to navigate them together and maintain (or regain) a sense of loving connection.

Psychiatrist and neuroscientist Amir Levine recommends the movie *Brooklyn*, which is about people who relate to each other predominantly in a securely attached way.[10] Another example of secure attachment is the mother-daughter relationship between Lorelai and Rory Gilmore in the TV series *Gilmore Girls*. And while their relationship may reflect a certain lack of parent-child boundaries, it mostly shows secure attachment. Of course, these are just a few options among thousands.

And because what you watch influences you, I also recommend reducing the number of dysfunctional, abusive, or otherwise violent movies you watch. I'm not talking about totally avoiding these; I'm just encouraging you to become more affiliated with what fosters healthy relationships—to nourish your secure attachment network with "nutritious food." What primes your awareness in that direction? Do the books you read and the shows you watch encourage secure attachment or something not so ideal for you and your family? If nothing else, it's worth contemplating and trying this for yourself. If you want more exposure to secure attachment, seek it out in your mentors, media, friends, and relationships. The rewards of secure attachment are certainly worth the effort.

To end this chapter on a positive note, try the following contemplation. If even for a few minutes, attend to what's going well in your life.

EXERCISE What's Working?

Take a moment to reflect on the qualities of secure attachment and the SAS offered in this chapter. Which of these are you already familiar with, and which are present in your life today? With whom do you (or did you) feel securely attached, and what practices are you engaging in to foster those healthy relationships? In other words, what's going right in your life already? If that's a difficult question to answer (for example, maybe very little of this resonates with you), then just focus on the elements in this chapter that call to you the most. For example, which of the SAS are you most excited about or interested in trying? Maybe it's more eye contact or longer hugs or simply watching more TV programs that reflect healthy relationships. Maybe you make an effort to respond more promptly to emails, texts, and calls. How might you be more expressive or protective if that is an issue for you? How might you practice enjoying alone time and learning to self-soothe if that is a challenge you face? How might you build more safety into your parenting or partnering? Maybe you hold your partner's hand more often and are more generous with your reassurances of love and commitment. What is it that you want to focus on going forward?

Whatever your answers to these questions are, I invite you to notice how your relationships shift as you bring these practices and skills to the forefront. Secure attachment is your birthright, and practicing the way it manifests will make it all the more prominent and evident in your life.

QUESTIONS TO ASSESS
FOR SECURE ATTACHMENT

- Do you want to be close to others, find it easy to connect, and expect relationships to go well?

- Do you feel relaxed most of the time with the people who are close to you?

- Do you transition between alone time and time together fluidly and without much difficulty?

- Do you and your partner apologize easily and work for win-win solutions to any conflicts that arise?

- Do you believe that people are basically good at heart?

- Is it important to you to meet the needs of the people who are close to you?

- Do you easily and clearly ask to have your own needs met?

- Are you present with your loved ones and free yourself from distractions when connecting?

- Do you work to maintain safety in your relationships, and do you protect those with whom you feel close?

- Do you look forward to spending time with your partner and friends?

- Are you affectionate with those with whom you feel close?

- Do you respect others' needs for privacy?

- How important are healthy boundaries to you?

- Do you leave when things are too off in a relationship, knowing there are other great options for fulfilling relationships?

- Do you make time to play regularly?

2

AVOIDANT ATTACHMENT

U p to this point, we've focused on secure attachment, beginning the journey with the ultimate goal in mind. I want to turn now to what we do when things don't go so well in our life. Specifically, I'm referring to attachment disruptions—the various styles of insecure attachment that so many of us live and struggle with. You'll see that I also like to use the term *attachment adaptation*, and that's for good reason. As babies, we need our parents to survive; we don't have any choice in the matter. We *adapt* according to whatever capacities they possess or lack. On a foundational level, we respond and grow according to whatever works and doesn't work. No matter where we end up in life (namely, whatever attachment style we embody), I think the fact that we adapted the best we could is worthy of respect and at least some level of appreciation for the dilemma each child must face. If we hit the jackpot, we may live in a family graced with secure attachment. If not, we have no choice but to adapt to the limitations of our caregivers, and we adapt in the way we can best maintain nourishment for our natural attachment needs, even if that paradoxically means that we shut down our need for connection.

We didn't have a lot of research on how children form attachment adaptations until the 1970s, when Mary Ainsworth conducted her "Strange Situation" studies. Ainsworth was a researcher and psychologist who had studied with John Bowlby. She devised a procedure that examined about one hundred families with children between the ages of twelve months and eighteen months. The kids were in a room with their mothers and a stranger, playing with few toys, and the researchers observed and catalogued what happened when the mother left for a while and then returned. Some kids became excited when their mother returned, hugging them or inviting them over to play. Many of the children displayed very little stress and reacted positively in this way. However, some of the children didn't respond like this at all. When their mother returned, they acted as if they didn't care, or they ignored their mother entirely and simply kept playing with their toys by themselves. The researchers originally thought that these kids were merely indifferent, but when they added in physiological measures, these particular children displayed lots of signs of stress. They were actually experiencing strong reactions to their mother coming and going, but they were acting in such a way to make those experiences invisible. In a way, they had shut down their normal reactions, and they were expending a lot of energy to do so.[1]

There's a lot more to these studies than I'll reference in this book, including the fact that follow-up research indicated that infants can display different attachment styles with their other caregivers. However, for the purposes of this chapter, I want to focus on the kids just described. Ainsworth labeled their style of insecure attachment *avoidant* because of the manner in which these children kept their distance and had stopped seeking connection from their mother. Their signal cry had adapted; in many cases, it was simply turned off.[2] When we see adults act this way, we view them as self-sufficient, dismissive, aloof, or disconnected, but this study indicates that there's a lot more going on than meets the eye. This style in adults is called Dismissive.

CONTRIBUTORS TO AVOIDANT ATTACHMENT

I once worked with a businessman from Chicago. Growing up, his mother was quite distressed and had difficulty being present and loving with him. She was, however, very committed to cleaning the house on a regular basis. My client, Harold, remembered being alone in his crib without toys, mobiles, or much of anything in the way of entertainment, while his mother vacuumed around him as if he weren't there. He grew up isolated in a tangible way and didn't receive the important contact necessary to establish a regulated nervous system. Harold came into treatment because he lacked the skills to connect to his wife. Sadly, this example illustrates a couple of the factors involved in the development of the avoidant adaptation in children that can continue into adulthood:

Isolation. Simply put, children might be left alone too much. Even when they're not utterly secluded or isolated, they don't grow up with enough face-to-face time with their caregivers.

Lack of Presence. Even when they are around, the parents aren't present enough. Caregivers might be physically present but psychologically and emotionally removed such that the child feels as if no one is home.

Task-Based Presence. Parents might be present with their kids only when they are trying to teach them something. Kids translate this type of presence as "I'm here for you, but only if you're practical or functional."

Absence of Touch. I've mentioned before just how important caring touch is to children. Unfortunately, far too many kids grow up without this. Children might have plenty of adults around them but still develop an avoidant adaptation without appropriate, compassionate physical contact. They suffer from "skin hunger."

Emotional Neglect. Emotional neglect means that caregivers aren't sensitive to the emotional needs of their children. Either kids don't receive a timely or quality response or they don't get adequate emotional nourishment overall. Their dominant experience is one of consistent nonresponsiveness.

Expressive Dissonance. Parents might use facial expressions that don't match their emotional states (smiling when angry or sad, for example). Kids who experience this in an ongoing way have difficulty expressing themselves authentically with coherent facial expressions, and they often have trouble understanding, interpreting, or sending appropriate social cues.

Disrupted Engagement. In some cases—for example, when young children are sick and unable to engage in typical attachment behaviors—children do not adequately stimulate secure attachment responses in their parents. This can also happen in the other direction, where the parent is physically unable to respond in a way that engages the child's secure attachment network.

Rejection. Unfortunately, some children suffer from outright rejection from their parents. Even if the rejection isn't always flavored with obvious hostility, it can still have a profound impact on kids, especially if it occurs regularly.

Once again: No matter what happens to us as children, we adapt to our caregivers. Through interacting with them and their nervous system, we internalize how we view relationships and form strategies for meeting our emotional and social needs. This is how we obtain the original relational blueprint I referred to in the introduction. If we reach out and are met with neglect or rejection, it's understandable that we will reduce our attachment-seeking behavior. And if our parents don't meet our emotional needs with quality responses, it's reasonable that we might begin to rely more and more on ourself. We become reactively autonomous. This differs from the normal developmental process of becoming increasingly able to do more things on our own as we grow up because there are some things children are not equipped to do or provide for themselves at such an early age. It's one thing to be self-sufficient as an adult, quite another to have to do so as a young child.

I take issue with some of the books written on attachment theory that state that people with avoidant adaptation don't want connection—that there's something about them that they don't need or want relationships. I don't think this is true at all. I believe that we all long for love and connection and that such longing comes directly from our secure attachment system, which is inherent in everyone—no matter our attachment style.

We might grow up in an environment where relationships aren't safe or nourishing, so we have trouble allowing ourself to become vulnerable with others. However, in no way does that mean that we don't want connection and closeness underneath. If avoidant, we can be disconnected from the longing to connect. As my clients have worked through their wounds of neglect, they find they want relationship just as much as everyone else; it's just a really big risk—and leaves us feeling incredibly vulnerable—to open up to others. But to reiterate what I've said multiple times before, secure attachment is possible for all of us. And those of us who adapted in an avoidant way are no exception.

WHAT AVOIDANT ATTACHMENT LOOKS LIKE

"Detached," "off in their own world," "insensitive," "cold," "standoffish," "lone wolf," "workaholic"—these are a just a few descriptors we typically associate with avoidant people. But let's take a closer look at how the avoidant adaptation manifests itself (especially in adulthood), as well as some of the reasons behind these expressions.

Relational Discomfort and Isolated Sense of Self

Understandably, when we grow up with an avoidance adaptation, we are often isolated from other people. Being alone can feel like the natural state, and we mature with a strong separate sense of self. We prefer to do things for ourself, as opposed to asking for help or joining others in mutual projects, or we form less problematic relationships with inanimate objects (possessions) or nonhuman friends (animals and plants). At times longing for others might surface and then we might not like being alone—it can even feel devastatingly painful at times—but we don't realize that there's another way of being.

We simply don't know what it's like to live in a comfortable relational field. Many avoidant people can feel like outcasts or alien—as if their level of isolation makes them a different type of being altogether. In some extreme cases, avoidant people may even refer to themselves as *it*, as if they were impersonal robots or machines.

Because our original relational blueprint tells us that relationships aren't nourishing, we grow up devaluing interpersonal connection. We typically don't reach out to others because we don't expect them to be there for us or meet our needs. If we grow up experiencing relationships as predominantly negative and painful, it makes sense that we wouldn't seek them out or rely on them as adults. In our implicit memory, being close to others was not a good experience. We might have a number of friendships, but few or none that actually involve deep, intimate relationship over a period of time. Sexually, we might prefer one-night stands or solo masturbation over longer-lasting intimate connections with others. And even when we do choose to be in relationship, we might have trouble expressing our commitment to our partner in a reliable, nourishing way.

We might not even miss people who are important to us when they're gone. We can feel a sense of relief when people physically leave us initially—for work, trips away, divorce, or even when they die—a temporary sort of "separation elation" as the pressure to connect is temporarily gone. And we may be quite unaware of the level of disconnection we live with until we start to heal. For avoidant people, the attachment system is underactivated. It's as if part of us is shut off because we didn't enjoy enough comfortable, nourishing connection when we were younger, particularly in the first couple of years of life.

However, beneath it all, we still yearn for connection, even if we live with an unspoken fear of rejection. For this reason, when someone with avoidant attachment opens up in a relationship, it can feel incredibly vulnerable. But just like anyone else, over time we can experience our innate secure attachment, especially when we find a nourishing partner or friend who offers reliable connection. We can learn to trust them and open up to the genuine care that's available in the relationship.

Dissociation

It can feel comfortable and normal for avoidant people to dissociate. We have deactivating strategies to ensure distance when the stress of connecting feels overwhelming. The originating neglect we experienced could have been so painful that the only way out was to "leave" through disconnection. Often those of us with the avoidant attachment style will distract ourselves with activities that promote disconnection from others—surfing the Internet, playing computer games, watching TV, even meditating. Sometimes avoidant people use these things to reground themselves and come back to a greater sense of presence, but far too often such activities only promote increased disembodiment. We might end up feeling calmer but simultaneously less connected to ourself and others.

For those of us who align with the avoidance adaptation, I suggest focusing a little more than we normally might on physical embodiment and emotional presence. For example, instead of turning to our typical means of coping (say, choosing to zone out on the computer for a while), we decide to engage with others and do our best to connect with them. Of course, approaching others can feel challenging to avoidant people, so it may be important in the beginning to make conscious decisions about when to do so and with whom until it feels natural. I suggest simply asking others for something you need (say, a glass of water or help with repairing something around the house) or sharing a story about your day.

If you are the partner of someone with the avoidant adaptation, do your best not to take their independence, dismissiveness, or dissociation too personally. Avoidants have reacted to the neglect or rejection they originally experienced by deactivating their attachment system. They withdraw and have learned to isolate. It takes a lot of energy to keep the brakes on their need for connection. It can be especially difficult for them to maintain a more intimate relationship unless they commit to learning secure attachment skills and do the work to heal and to connect.

And if you identify with this attachment style, try out the following practice in order to challenge some of your deeply held (mostly unconscious) feelings regarding connection.

EXERCISE   Practice Joint Attention

Those of us who grew up with the avoidant adaptation usually prefer
parallel attention activities when in the company of others that don't
involve their participation: playing video games or watching movies,
for example. This means that there's very little interaction or mutual
engagement while we both participate in the activity at hand. So the
suggestion here is to try a joint attention activity (covered to some degree
in the previous chapter). Choose something that will help you include the
other person in your experience as it unfolds. Whatever it is—dining out,
hiking, going for a scenic drive, or visiting a museum—do your best to
connect with your partner or friend as you experience the activity together.
Hang in there long enough to find out how doing such a thing can
actually nourish you. You don't have to make a continuous effort for the
duration of the outing, but try your best to be a little more interactive and
communicative than you normally might.

If your partner is avoidant, you might notice things they do unconsciously and unintentionally that create distance you would like to
bridge. For example, two friends—Dee Dee and Shelly—often walk
around the city together. Shelly always walks ahead of her friend. Dee
Dee understands this is not meant to hurt her, but she frequently suggests that they stop at the local food trucks and art galleries, so they
can literally catch up and be together to share the experiences. What
Shelly and Dee Dee enjoyed individually is brought into communal
joint attention, which invites greater closeness, mutuality, and connection. This serves to immerse the more avoidant Shelly into easy
connection, and the two gradually find they can trust each other to be
there in a kindhearted way that leads to easier connection in the future.

Difficulty with Eye Contact

When we look out into the world as a child at our caregivers, we're
seeking evidence of love, appreciation, and presence. We look into the
eyes of our loved ones to mirror who we are. We build our sense of self

and personality from their mirroring, whether it's accurate or not. For example, we may be quite intelligent, but if a parent looks at us as if we're stupid, we may take on that identity until hopefully we peel it off later in life. If we see love in our parents' eyes, on the other hand, we are mirrored into seeing ourself as loveable, and we also learn how to be loving.

When we're met with a gaze that communicates absence, anger, critique, or rejection, it's understandable that eye contact will be an issue for us growing up. We may expect to see belittling, anger, rejection, or even hatred whenever we catch someone's eye. That kind of negative mirroring may add insult to injury in that we come to see ourself as inadequate, unlovable, wrong, stupid, shameful, or worse. Far too many of us didn't receive that beam gleam I talked about in the last chapter, or we simply didn't get enough looks that said, "You're special to me" or "I love you" or "You're lovable." If eye contact is something we wanted to turn away from as children, that can leave a significant wound we'll want to pay attention to as adults. Sometimes kids develop an ability to appear like they're maintaining eye contact, but what they've actually learned to do is focus on the other person's nose, teeth, or chin. It's hard to tell when someone is "dodging the bullet" of eye contact with you instead of looking directly into your eyes. A lot of us do this without even being aware of it.

I once worked with a couple who were trying their best to connect, but they kept encountering all sorts of challenges grounded in their attachment adaptations. Jim wanted more eye contact with Sally, but it proved difficult for her to respond in this way. She experienced shame instead of being able to take in his look of love toward her. Shame moves us to gaze avert, which means we look down and away, and both Jim and Sally needed to understand this as part of Sally's ongoing recovery. When she tried to maintain eye contact, it stressed her out and led to her shutting down. It's important to give permission for a person to look at you and look away as they need to—to not force eye contact, especially when shame is dominant. Even though Jim's gaze was loving and supportive, it was overwhelming for Sally to try to meet him like that. So instead of focusing on eye contact, I suggested that they try hugging. When you hug, you typically don't have eye contact with the other person; it's just a nice way to feel safe and physically connected. This worked a lot better for Sally as a starting point for more relaxed connection on her way back across the bridge toward secure attachment with Jim.

If eye contact is difficult for you, make sure you practice self-compassion and patience. If you do want to try to connect more in this way, don't turn the practice into a bare-knuckled staring contest. It's okay to look away and take breaks. It's natural for us to look at others and occasionally look away; it helps us to regulate and orient ourself. So if you want to engage in corrective practices like the one in the following exercise, pace yourself. The idea isn't to make things more difficult and learn how to endure that discomfort, but to open a doorway that enables you to access all of the blessings of secure attachment. In other words, you want this to gradually become a uniquely positive experience for you.

EXERCISE **Kind Eyes**

Depending on what it brings up for you, feel free to engage in this practice for just a little bit or for as long as feels right and nourishing. Begin by taking a seat, relaxing into your body, and taking a couple of deep breaths. Keep your eyes open or closed—whatever comes easier for you. Now imagine looking out into the world and seeing kind eyes looking back at you. Maybe the eyes belong to your lover or your kindly grandfather, your children, dog, or even the Dalai Lama or Pope Francis. Choose someone who can offer you their kind eyes effortlessly, even if it's someone imaginary. If you have trouble visualizing kind eyes in this way, gather photographs of people you know or others (even strangers) who have this beam gleam of kindness coming out of their eyes. Look into their eyes and feel their boundless acceptance and caring as much as you can comfortably take in. One of my clients, Ted, made a photo album on his smartphone of everyone he loves. Ted calls it his "bubble of connection" and takes a look at it whenever he needs to feel less alone or more supported.

Now simply notice how it feels to receive this type of gaze. What happens in your body as you look into these kind eyes shining back at you? Noticing this type of kindness or openness is the first step, and it can sometimes prove quite challenging. Take in as much of this gentleness and compassion as possible. Reach out for or drink in the kindness with your eyes. What do your eyes feel like in this moment? Do the muscles around your eyes relax? If you feel increased tension, that's okay too; just imagine your eyes relaxing back into their sockets—very softly, as if on a hammock or pillow. What's the experience like in your shoulders, your neck? Get curious about what various parts of your body feel like. Just gently check it out. We cannot predict if relief will come first or if residue from old wounds may intrude. Take time to experience your feelings and reactions, no matter which direction the exercise takes you, and feel free to revisit this exercise with support from others at any time.

Self-Regulation and the Importance of Transitions

Avoidant people are accustomed to being alone and deeply involved in their own internal experience. For this reason, interacting with others can sometimes prove challenging. If you approach someone with an avoidance adaptation while they're still involved in their internal exploration, they might respond a little roughly or curtly, and it can feel to you as if the abruptness comes out of nowhere. I assure you: it doesn't.

Again, I know it can prove difficult, but do your best to not take this kind of response too personally. If you think about how difficult it is for avoidant people to surface from an isolated experience—one that doesn't involve anyone but themselves—it might help a little. It's understandable to feel rejected when someone with the avoidant adaptation responds in such a dismissive manner, but we can also keep in mind that their curt response is part of how they adjust to coming back to connecting with other people.

Avoidant people actually do want connection; they just need more transition time to take the pressure off and ease the way for a smoother path to connection. If you have a partner who is avoidant, I suggest offering them that space. For example, you could say something like, "I'd love to take you out to dinner and connect with you in about thirty minutes or so. How much time do you need to get ready for us to go out and enjoy a nice evening together?" That's a useful way to signal respect to them and give them the opportunity they need to make the necessary shift. It's a bit like scuba diving. If you're hundreds of feet below the surface, you need to come up slowly, or else you can get the bends—decompression sickness. Avoidant people need to take their time to decompress the stress they feel about being with others, or everything goes haywire. There's nothing wrong with this; it's just how it is.

Moving from intense internal focus to a more relational focus is hard work, and if you're an avoidant person, it will help you to remember that you need time to transition from one state to the other. You may need to practice taking a deep breath and challenging yourself to approach your partner or others; make the first move more to initiate being together. Invite your loved ones into conversations and joint activities even for short periods of time at the beginning. You may need time to adjust at first, so remember to ask for it—for example, "I am happy to join you and can be ready in twenty minutes" or "I have to think about going to the party and will get back to you on Wednesday" or "I'll go to the party with you, but I need you to let me play pool with the guys for a while or leave early if I need to."

Trouble Recognizing Personal Needs

It's common for avoidant people to not recognize or reflect on the unique difficulties of their upbringing. In general, they might be more future oriented, and when they do discuss the past, they might come across as vague or somewhat dismissive of their personal struggles. It can often appear that they're not conscious of the neglect they suffered or the fact that their emotional needs were consistently unmet when they were young children. In a sense, they're disconnected from their past. They might also frame their childhood in a positive light (for example, "I had everything I needed. I couldn't really have asked for more"). Part of the challenge for people with the avoidant adaptation who are interested in regaining a sense of secure attachment is to excavate those original longings for connection, longings that were not met. And we absolutely want that to be a positive experience for them.

Please keep this in mind if you're the partner of an avoidant person and do your best to avoid adding more critique or rejection to their already entrenched association with personal connection.

As avoidant people who did not have our needs met in childhood, we can sometimes be dismissive of our own personal needs as adults. We might not even be aware of them, especially if we aren't prone to self-reflection. We had to reckon with ongoing distress on our own at an inappropriate age, which might cause us to inhibit some natural responses as adults. And even if we are aware of our own needs, we can be prone to rejecting the attempts of loved ones to help and support us. If we don't accept help from others—either thinking that we don't need anything from them or that they won't help us in the way that we need it—we miss out on their support and also rob them of their real need to express generosity to us. Either way, we diminish the opportunity for connection and authentic exchange.

If this sounds familiar to you, practice asking another person for help and support as an experiment. Even if they don't come through perfectly, notice what it feels like when you allow yourself to be cared for and supported. Doing so is good for both of you, and experiencing that mutuality is an important step toward secure attachment.

We can become so identified with self-sufficiency that it can be difficult to understand why other people aren't the same. Their dependency can confuse us, leading us to be a little suspicious about their motives or even to feel superior to them because we believe they rely on others so much. If we pulled ourself up by our bootstraps, why can't they? For this reason, as avoidants, we can struggle to express empathy and have trouble recognizing and honoring the very real needs of our partners or children and can view them as overly dependent or even as a burden when they are simply expressing natural needs.

As avoidant people, we tend to identify with some of the more glorified aspects of our culture—namely, independence, autonomy, and self-determination. These can be admirable qualities in the proper context, but the larger reality is that we're all interdependent with each other, and this fact is certainly evident when it comes to relationships. Interdependence means that we can take care of ourself with the help of others, and others can achieve an interconnected autonomy with our involvement and support. To truly explore ourself, we need one another; to be together deeply, we need to take care of ourself. Couples therapist and author Marion Solomon writes about "positive dependency."[3] Dependency gets a bad rap, like it's a derogatory word, but dependency can be generative, connective, and healthy. It's important that we learn to meet our own needs, of course, but we also need to receive support from others and offer to meet their needs, as well. Doing so makes relationships valuable and rewarding.

Left-Brain Orientation

Kids who grow up without much support, presence, emotional awareness, or connection to others can become more left-brain oriented. This means that they're more factual, analytical, and logical. This type of orientation is extremely valuable, and there are many important interpersonal skills related to this part of the brain.

However, what we often see in conjunction with a hyperdeveloped left side of the brain is a lack of emotional warmth or depth, which may signify a lack of input from the right hemisphere. People like this can also be a bit out of touch with their intuitive and interpersonal nature, which means that they can sometimes miss or misinterpret important social messages and cues, even to the point of assigning false motives to other people. Left-brain-dominated people are focused on a particular set of facts. Because of the way their brain processed early experiences, avoidants sometimes are unable to contact early memories, and when they do talk about their childhood, they might remember impersonal facts such as where they went to kindergarten, exactly where they sat in the classroom, and what their teacher's name was, but they might not have much sense of what it felt like to be there in an embodied or emotional way. These memories can be quite vivid, but they can feel impersonal because they don't entail much emotional content. This is just one way that an overdevelopment of the left brain (or underdevelopment of the right) can reveal itself. The right brain is much more emotional, intuitive, relationship-focused, and attachment-oriented. Our goal here isn't to diminish the gifts that come with a left-brain orientation, but to attempt to balance things in a way that wasn't possible during the avoidant person's childhood.

Bias Toward Action

As I mentioned above, people with the avoidant adaptation reveal a lot about themselves in how they talk about their past. They might not be forthcoming or descriptive, and it can feel like you have to pull words out of them to get a picture of what their childhood was like. Part of the reason for this is that avoidant people typically didn't have people around in childhood to nourish their ability and willingness to communicate. Avoidants can be extremely concise and factual, typically employing fewer words and without the richness of emotion or colorful nuance. In the process, they may not provide enough information for others to fully understand what they are trying to communicate.

On the flip side, avoidant people can have trouble understanding the value that other people derive from communicating with what they consider to be excessive words, and they regularly feel impatient when others relay personal stories, especially when they feel overwhelmed with too much description and detail. If this is true for you, try experimenting with sharing more of your personal stories with a few more details and notice if you can find any emotional nuances. Listen with more attention, presence, and patience when other people share. This can feel unnatural, almost like learning a foreign language. The rewards are worth it, though, as sharing in this way is one of the foundations of satisfying relationships.

If you're in a relationship with someone more oriented to avoidant, you may want to practice being more concise in your storytelling so as not to lose them in the loquaciousness. It's hard for them to process and integrate what feels like an overdose of information. Ideally, good storytellers flavor their tales with lots of emotion and nuance and with enough information so that listeners can follow the flow easily and feel interested and engaged without excessive detail.

Instead of being aligned with detailed communication and verbal processing, avoidant people are often much more work oriented and task focused. Again, there are significant advantages to this.

These people tend to be efficient and productive; of all of us, they're the best at remaining focused on work projects. They are expert at taking on projects by themselves and can find being on a team limiting, as they feel the relational processing or decision-making by committee frustrating or unnecessary. That being said, doers contribute uniquely to our society and our personal lives. However, if you're in relationship with an avoidant person who always puts their work or career first, it can feel painful or neglectful. All too often, your needs are unacknowledged and unmet. When work takes most of the focus, relationships take a back seat, and we're after a more balanced relationship between the two.

As we move toward secure attachment, we come to value relationships more, which means that we devote more time, energy, and presence to them. It isn't that we stop working or doing all the tasks we find necessary to perform, just that we commit a bit more focus to the relationships that can make life enjoyable and rewarding.

Gesture Inhibition

As I mentioned earlier, avoidant people can tend toward dissociation, and this propensity can sometimes manifest in physical ways. If physical connection was regularly disappointing or the absence of it painful when we were small, we can grow up being inhibited in our physical gestures that are designed to promote personal connection (reaching out for hugs, leaning in for support, using a "come hither" gesture, or sending an invitation to connect through our eyes) or in responding to the same in others. It might even be difficult to greet or welcome others when they approach us. See if you can practice approaching others more often and extending a welcome when approached by others.

I once worked with a woman, Sandra, who suffered significant trauma during her birth. Her mother went through a complicated caesarean section, and the many post-op procedures kept Sandra from her mother for an extended time. Sadly, her mother experienced extreme postpartum depression and died when Sandra was only a year and a half old. Sandra's father experienced incredible grief that manifested in even less physical connection for Sandra. Essentially, Sandra lost both parents early. She had no one to connect to or bond with and grew up in a relational vacuum.

I worked with Sandra in a group setting. We discovered that she lacked much sense of her body from the waist up. As she processed the grief of losing her mother so young, Sandra gradually became more embodied in her torso. With the help of a warm and compassionate group of peers, she was able to physically feel the absence of her mother and father, as if her heart had been scooped out of her chest. Later, Sandra was also able to connect to the times when her father was present and supportive. As she dove into those experiences, her body began to lean to the side. She was leaning so far to the side of her chair that I began to worry she might fall. Sandra said, "This is getting painful. I don't know why, but my body wants to do this." She refused help from anyone in the group (recall that avoidant people have difficulty asking for help). Sandra was trying to keep her head up, but it was tilted so off-center that it became too painful to endure. Eventually, Sandra gained a crucial insight into what was going on. "Oh," she said, "I'm trying to do this alone. I'm trying to do this all by myself."

With support, Sandra was able to invite someone to help her—one of the talented body workers in the group. This person went over to Sandra, Sandra leaned into her, and Sandra's whole body relaxed. She just melted into this other person like a child does over the shoulder of a loving parent. This went on for some time, and Sandra took in the nourishment. It was like watching a physical restoration of secure attachment in action, and it was beautiful.

This re-embodiment continued in other ways. Earlier, Sandra's hands had been splayed—her tensed fingers reaching out stiffly in an uncomfortable way that's indicative of in-utero stress. Now her hands looked different, more relaxed and natural, and one of her arms reached up as if stroking the air. This was a foreign gesture to Sandra, and it felt to her that her arm was doing it on its own. But as she explored the movement further, Sandra identified it as a kind of reaching out. "It doesn't feel strange or futile to me," she said. "I'm reaching out, and it feels like someone's there." She was in direct communication with the secure attachment system. Even though Sandra experienced so much emptiness and physical absence as a child, she could now connect to something direct, potent, and nourishing. It was an entirely new physiological experience for her. Her nervous system was newly adapting—away from avoidance and toward secure attachment, which was there the whole time.

The attachment work I do with others can be unbelievably powerful and mysterious in this way. We all have these capacities, and we're often far more ready to embrace them than we know. We simply have to find a way to allow secure attachment to arise, be supported, and express itself. Crucial to this process is being in an environment in which we can enjoy a better response than we experienced as children. When that happens, we have the chance to enjoy the corrective experiences that make us more familiar and aligned with secure attachment.

When we enter the world from an avoidant perspective, it can feel like we never really landed, or that we came in with one foot on the planet and one foot off. Whatever complications that met us early on made it difficult for us to become a fully embodied human committed to the experience of being here. Many of us suffer from wounds of isolation like Sandra, and the following three-part exercise is meant to counter that sense of impersonal neglect. Ideally, this practice will help you experience the possibility of what it's like to be welcomed and celebrated from the very beginning of your life.

EXERCISE **Welcome to the World**

Part One—Your Ideal Scenario

I want you to imagine the ideal scenario for your entry into this life. Using visualization, drawing, or photographs, create the best possible birth experience you can imagine for yourself. Perhaps it involves music, the perfect nursery, scenes of your delighted parents making plans for your arrival, flowers, waterfalls, whatever. Take some time imagining it in detail. Allow yourself to let go and dive deep into this experience of being welcomed into the world in a way that feels supportive, nourishing, and special. Some of my clients have wanted to be born into warm, loving hands or to arrive in a field full of flowers surrounded by their horses softly nuzzling them. Some wanted their mother to hold them skin to skin or for all their relatives to sing lullabies, welcoming them into the family. Write down what you see and experience about your optimal arrival or share it with a friend or loved one. Feel the sensations, emotions, thoughts, and meanings open up or shift.

Part Two—Your Loving Community

Who are the people there to greet you? Include all the people who made a positive contribution to you from any period of your life. Maybe it's your mother, father, siblings, favorite grandparent, or some distant, benevolent ancestor; perhaps it's your nanny or best friend from preschool. It could be a favorite childhood teacher, spiritual guide, beloved pet, or first crush in middle school. It could be the partner you're with now or your closest circle of friends. Gather these people around you in the scenario you created in part one. Allow them to show up—as many as you'd like—and have them greet you as you come into the world. Look around at all of them. Let them introduce themselves to you. Make contact with each of them, look into their faces, and feel the warmth and connection. Don't worry about timelines here; just gather your community of support and enjoy the experience.

Even if you were born in terrible circumstances, use this exercise to see that there's light at the end of the tunnel. Despite your difficult beginnings, know that there will be people in your future who will bring you ample doses of uncompromised love and support. It may help alleviate some of the early pain and suffering by knowing there are people on their way who want to connect with you, welcome you, and empower you. Take in as much of their caring attention as you possibly can. Write about this community or put together an album of photos that you can easily pick up (or look at on your phone) to access these people whenever you want. Think of this as your personal album of allies or your own bubble of connection.

Part Three—Honoring Your Gift

In this perfect version of your birth, surrounded by these wonderful people, think about what you bring to the world. What's your contribution to humanity? What's your special talent? What is it that you bring to this community of souls that no one else can offer? Whatever it is, imagine that the people in your loving circle recognize and celebrate your specific talent, gift, or contribution. They immediately understand what it is that you have to offer; they receive it fully and support you wholeheartedly. They welcome your gift and acknowledge you. What's this like, to be seen accurately for the essence of who you are and what you bring? What are your sensations and feelings as you imagine this recognition and attunement?

You may want to do one part of this exercise in a separate session and return to do another part at some other time. It's also great to repeat these practices if you can. Take as much time as you need with each part. If the exercise becomes too intense or difficult at any point, take a break and take care of yourself. When you feel ready to return to the exercise, feel free to return to the parts you'd like to savor the most. Pay attention to what happens to your emotional and physical being when you do so. What kind of thoughts show up? What do you notice? For many people, this exercise can be deeply corrective. If nothing else, I hope you get a little sense of what it's like to be genuinely recognized, welcomed, and loved. Seek help or guidance from friends, your partner, or a trusted therapist as you wish.

DESERT OR OASIS

I want to end this chapter with a story about a documentary I saw a few years ago. It's about a desert where it rains only once every seven years. Between these infrequent rains, the desert experiences incredible drought. The earth gets drier and drier, cracking and fragmenting everywhere, just like cement does over time. As the time passes in this desert, the animals who live there either leave or die, and the plants dry up and decay. After a few years, it looks like there's no possible way that anything could survive more than a couple of days there; the landscape is just so parched and bare.

But then the rains eventually come again. At first, the water just floats on top of the dry earth, but after a while it begins to soak in.

Surprisingly, tiny green shoots start to peek up in the gradually softening earth because—as it turns out—there were seeds lying dormant there the whole time. The shoots are nourished by the rain, they grow larger and more numerous, and before you know it, the whole desert floor is covered with greenery. Then, gradually, small rivulets appear everywhere, then larger creeks. The vegetation becomes lusher; flowers and bushes start to grow. And before long, this place that was so barren and lifeless and sere is now a thriving oasis. There are seeds and fruit now, birds fly in from everywhere in the region, and animals come to live there too. It's a flourishing, lush garden—a paradise of life in all its forms.

I hope the analogy is evident. We're just like that dry, thirsty desert. When the environment is right, all the natural ingredients we need for life and vitality surface and bloom, and we absorb and enjoy the nourishing rain. It doesn't matter who you are or what you've experienced; your richness, fullness, and capacity for connection and relationship are all right there. And as soon as you encounter the right situation and open to it, your inclination for authentic love and intimacy will flower. Your core is intact! Your essence is alive!

If you identify with avoidant attachment and wish to face some of your particular struggles head on, I encourage you to revisit the exercises I've presented in this chapter. They might prove challenging to you, but I promise that the rewards—enhanced empathy, improved social interactions, better adaptations to stress, increased connection and intimacy, heightened somatic awareness, and so on—are more than worth it.

QUESTIONS TO ASSESS FOR AVOIDANT ATTACHMENT

- Are close relationships difficult for you?

- Does closeness cause you to create distance afterward?

- Do you find it difficult to relax with your partner in your intimate relationship??

- Do you feel inexplicably stressed when people approach you physically?

- How difficult is it for you to reach out and ask for help?

- Do you have trouble knowing or asking for what you need?

- Do you struggle to maintain eye contact?

- Do you prefer to work alone instead of with others?

- Would you rather be with others or engage in solo activities?

- Do you often judge others for not being more self-sufficient?

- Do you find emotional, effusive, or dramatic people annoying?

- Which is easier to do: to think about issues that are important to you or to express how you feel about these topics to others?

- When you have lost an important relationship in the past, did you feel an initial wave of relief or happiness? Was that wave eventually followed by polar opposite feelings like depression or despair?

- Do you prefer relationships with animals or objects over relationships with people?

- How important is your career and work life in comparison to your personal relationships?

- Do you feel more available and connected to your exes after you break up, when the pressure is off?

- Do you feel there's a perfect someone out there who you haven't met yet and that it is easier to search for that fantasy bond than enjoy and commit to the person you're actually with?

3

AMBIVALENT ATTACHMENT

n *Attached: Create Your Perfect Relationship with the Help of the Three Attachment Styles*, Amir Levine and Rachel Heller refer to a young couple: Georgia, with an ambivalent-anxious attachment style, and Henry, with an avoidant one.[1] They were bickering about a recurring issue in their marriage when the authors interviewed them. Henry felt judged and overwhelmed by Georgia's incessant demands; Georgia felt like she did the heavy lifting in the relationship. She felt alone because Henry never had time for her during his workday, and he rarely responded to her messages. As they understood each other's attachment paradigms, Henry realized that by ignoring Georgia's attempts to contact him, being abrupt when she called, or ridiculing her needs, he was hurting her and their relationship. Georgia realized that by complaining and being demanding, she was pushing Henry away, when what she wanted was to be closer. She also came to understand that Henry did think about her often during the day but that his busy schedule made it hard to stay in contact. Together they found an inspired solution: they created a prewritten text with an "I'm thinking of you" type message that Henry could send Georgia anytime he thought of her—quickly and easily. This reduced Georgia's anxiety and worry about the relationship, and Henry felt less resentful of what he had considered to be nagging and interrupting his work. Now, instead of fighting, they could meet after work without tension or hostility and enjoy their time together.

THE ROLE OF OBJECT PERMANENCE
AND OBJECT CONSTANCY

One way to get to the heart of ambivalent attachment is to understand the concepts of object permanence and object constancy and how these can get disrupted when we're quite young. Until we're about eighteen months old or so, we don't have much sense of object permanence, which means that when a person leaves the room, from the perspective of an infant, they might as well have dematerialized. That person—the object in question—has simply vanished. But as we grow older and develop object permanence, we can create an image or feeling of that person when they're not physically present, so when our mother leaves us to go to the kitchen, we have a sense that she's still there in a tangible way, and we have some confidence that she'll eventually come back. At about the same time in our development, we start to gain a sense of object constancy. That means that when our mother comes back into the room from being away in the kitchen, we understand that she's roughly the same person who left us a couple of minutes ago. The object in question has not been replaced with something else. Our ability to detect object permanence and object constancy enables us to develop a sense of continuity with our primary attachment figures over time. It's somewhat difficult to develop bonds with people without these abilities.

When we experience inconsistent or unreliable caregiving, it can thwart our ability to establish object permanence and object constancy. As children, when we don't know who's going to show up or whether our needs are going to be met, we grow up with a particular type of anxiety. The on-and-off attachment experience encourages us to feel doubtful and insecure. It's important to point out that many of us who have ambivalent attachment actually did receive lots of love and high-quality interactions with our parents; it's just that our relationship with our caregivers was marked by unpredictability and inconsistency. Things might have been okay or even good for a while, but they didn't stay that way in a reliable fashion, or we never knew as children which way things were going to go. Maybe we'd get what we needed, but maybe we wouldn't. It was like flipping a coin or playing a slot machine: here and there our attempts to connect would pay off with presence and love, but not in a trustworthy way. Accordingly, children with this type of caregiving grow up with a lot of associated stress.

As I've said elsewhere, parents with unresolved attachment injuries tend to pass their wounds on to their children, and this can certainly be the case with ambivalent attachment. As any mother or father will tell you, parenthood presents endless opportunities to trigger old patterns and hurts, most of the time without conscious recognition. In a very real way, an injury to the parent becomes an injury to the child. That's why it's so helpful that those of us with wounds related to consistency get to experience more reassurance about commitment, permanence, and reliability in our relationships. This chapter— particularly the exercises you'll find here—are intended to do just that.

Some other relational contributors that create insecurity for those with ambivalent attachment include the following:

> **Insufficient Co-regulation.** As you'll recall from chapter one, children who grow up securely attached tend to have parents who allow them to flow through various emotional states while remaining present and supportive. People with ambivalent attachment didn't receive this type of predictable care, which means their *affect modulation*— that is, their ability to navigate their internal emotional terrain—wasn't met with their parents' presence or consistent receptivity. This explains why ambivalents rely so heavily on others to regulate their feelings. Since they never received consistent or reliable interactive regulation from their parents, they have yet to develop sufficient self-regulation that developmentally builds on successful co-regulation, so they reach out to others to fill the original need. Sometimes they reject help, however, because having what they want or need may quiet their signal cry, but that very satisfaction threatens the ambivalent's survival because the next thing they expect is abandonment.

> **Interrupted Regulation.** In addition to the factors mentioned above, ambivalent attachment has been linked

to *interrupted regulation* on the part of primary caregivers. Interrupted regulation occurs when a child is trying to relax and calm themselves during a moment of high-quality attention and love by the parent, but the parent suddenly disrupts the experience without any warning. In other words, the child has relaxed into the relationship to regulate or receive nurturance, connection, and love, and the parent does the one thing that most endangers the child's ability to do so. This tendency typically points to a parent's preoccupation with their own attachment wounds, an injury suffered from their own parents that is easily transmitted to their child. Understandably, this type of exchange can disturb a child and promote relational anxiety. When adults suffer ambivalent attachment it is referred to as preoccupied.

Overstimulation. When children are learning to regulate themselves, they typically require lots of space to find their own rhythm and to develop healthy boundaries. If a parent intrudes into this space or tries to maintain constant connection, it can be detrimental to the child's development. ABC's *World News Now* featured the work of clinical professor of medical psychology Beatrice Beebe in a 2011 program that examines patterns between mothers and their infants. Because mothers have their own agendas and needs, they often ignore or fail to notice important signals from their kids that indicate the need for space—putting their hands up in front of their face, turning their face away, and so on. When mothers continue to stimulate their children despite these signs, a "chase and dodge" dynamic can ensue: the mother presses in more, and the infant doubles down on their attempts for space. The mother can feel as if the child doesn't love her, and the infant suffers from the overstimulation.[2] No matter our age, it's normal that we need to take a break from eye contact or physical presence after a period of intense interpersonal contact in order to regulate ourself.

When we learn more about attachment dynamics—those of ourself and others—and we apply that knowledge compassionately, we are able to foster secure attachment in relationships that may have been previously fraught with anxiety, insecurity, or habitual disengagement.

WHAT AMBIVALENT ATTACHMENT LOOKS LIKE

Just as avoidant people are typically associated with some fairly challenging qualities, adults with the ambivalent adaptation are sometimes denigrated as "needy," "clingy," "oversensitive," "controlling," "high-maintenance," or "high-strung." Here too, I want to move beyond judgmental language to take a closer look at what's going on with ambivalent people, as well as some ways to soothe some of the more difficult things that come along with living with this adaptation. Ambivalently attached folks really want a relationship so their attachment system is full on. They need more help to calm the overactivation, which is usually a bit easier than for the avoidants, who need to lift the brake against connection in order to uncover possible longing to be in relationship.

Departure Stress

I want to revisit Amir Levine and Rachel Heller's somewhat stereotypical example of the notably anxious wife. Consider how different her experience is from someone who lives with the avoidant attachment style. Avoidants regularly experience *approach stress*. Even with people they love, they can feel anxiety when people physically approach them, probably due to being hurt by their primary caregivers or simply being left alone too much as a child. As a result, people with avoidant attachment can sometimes come across as cold, walled off, distant, and even rejecting. The opposite is true for those of us with the ambivalent attachment style. Our anxiety can fire up whenever loved ones leave us, even if for something routine like going to work for the day or a brief outing to the gym. Ambivalent people tend to feel upset when alone and not in close proximity to the important people in their life. They might be high-functioning and in contact with their secure attachment network when in the presence of their relationship partner, but as soon as their loved one leaves, they begin to mistrust the connection. I have a friend who confides that she feels tremendous anxiety and a sense of abandonment each night when her boyfriend rolls over (that is, physically turns away) to fall asleep, even if they have spent a significant amount of time connected and cuddling beforehand. She goes through this painful experience with him on a regular basis, no matter how intimately connected they might have been just moments before.

Try to keep this in mind if you are the partner, parent, or child of someone with the ambivalent adaptation. Saying goodbye can prove extremely difficult for them in ways that might not make sense to you. Try to be as sensitive as you can to their transitional stress and try offering them words of encouragement or reassurance to show them that you recognize their difficulty. I have a friend who tells his daughter, "I will hold you in my heart, where I keep my love for you, every day," whenever he goes on a business trip.

Proximity Seeking and Relational Hyperfocus

We can guess that mothers like those in Beatrice Beebe's "chase and dodge" example grew up in a way that fostered ambivalence. Children with inconsistent parenting can easily become overly focused on others, especially their primary caregiver, because they live with a fear that the world of relationships is shaky and erratic. It makes sense that these children would want to maintain constant contact and display behavior we typically associate (with a particularly negative connotation) with clinginess. This type of proximity seeking is much more marked than in someone who grows up with secure attachment, understandably. If your self-regulatory functions aren't well developed, you will constantly look to others to down regulate, or calm, your overactivated nervous system and oversensitive attachment system. Stan Tatkin calls this "external regulation."[3] It isn't interactive regulation because it's marked by a lack of mutuality or reciprocity.

People with a high degree of ambivalence can become so focused on the perceived slights or nuances of relationships around them that they may have trouble focusing on work. They can even run into trouble when they focus so much on what is happening emotionally or interpersonally on the team that they fail to get their job done. When ambivalents are so focused on their personal relationships and compelled by their attachment wounds, their creativity and curiosity can become diminished, their careers can suffer, and their sense of contributing to their community or the larger society gets curtailed. Additionally, when we are overfocused on other people—their actions (or lack of actions), their presence (or lack of presence), and their love (or absence of love)—we become so emerged in the vicissitudes of others that we lose contact with ourself. The right brain takes over, and we lose a much-needed connection to the wisdom of the left hemisphere. Sometimes this type of relational hyperfocus can lead ambivalent people to give and give and give to their partners, seemingly without an end to their flexibility and generosity. Unfortunately, this type of generosity is not always authentic, and people with the ambivalent adaptation will sometimes use what looks like altruism in unconsciously manipulative ways. We need to understand this dynamic compassionately, as they are attempting to stabilize the relationship. There is a gift here, too. Remember the avoidant is so task focused they can be relied upon to get the job done. Here the ambivalent, although at times hypersensitive, docs have a highly developed sense of "other" and can readily solve emotional entanglements or help get essential needs met.

When we're not able to self-soothe and aren't connected to who we are and what's going on with us—that is, our important needs and wants—then it's only natural that we'll continue the cycle of reaching out to connect with others and behaving in ways designed to charm or please them. Unfortunately, this pattern doesn't work very well. When we rely on others to an exaggerated degree, we can't establish a sense of desired connection no matter what the other person does. No matter how loving or perfect they are, this will never bring us back to ourself. As ambivalently attached people, we lose contact with ourself and reach out to others to get ourself back, but we end up abandoning ourself in the process. This is a significant dilemma for those of us with ambivalent attachment: relying on so much external input fosters continued overdependence, loss of control, and even more self-abandonment.

As I've stated elsewhere, it's important that we learn to self-soothe in combination with regulating with others. Here's one of my favorite exercises, which uses the wisdom and gifts of our body to help us learn to regulate and soothe on our own.

EXERCISE   Physical Grounding

When we move our joints with awareness, we gain proprioceptive awareness (the internal sense of how our body is positioned and moves). This practice will help you foster a stronger sense of self merely by feeling more into your own body. Try this out: Find a relaxing place to sit, take a few moments of silence, and start by feeling into the physical sensations of your feet. Rotate your ankles a little, wiggle your toes, and move the various bones of your feet. What's that like? How many sensations can you identify and get in touch with as you're doing this?

When you feel like you've gained some sense of connection here, try bringing your awareness higher up in your body. Rotate your ankles and move your knees around. Rotate your knees in and out and notice how those motions affect your hips. Feel as many sensations as you can in your knees, upper legs, and hips. Now turn your torso a little to the left and then to the right. Notice all the sensations in your spine. After doing this for a while, try straightening your spine as if a string is pulling you up into the sky, anchoring you in the clouds. Feel your vertebrae move and note how they support your head. Twist your torso from side to side. Try to get in touch with the different parts of your spine and feel how the vertebrae work together to keep you upright. Now turn your attention to all the little movements in your neck and upper spine. Let your head turn slowly from side to side, opening your eyes to see where you are in time and space. Look all around you to notice your surroundings and scan your body for sensations at the same time.

This practice activates the hippocampus and lets you know that you're right here, right now. Because our implicit memory is so powerful, it's sometimes easy for us to get lost in our early feelings or sensations when something—usually in relationship—triggers our early attachment patterning. This could be something as simple as your partner going out of town and forgetting to tell you they arrived safely, causing you to feel anxious and worried. When something like this happens, it helps to ground your body in the present moment.

Keep going. Let your shoulders relax and feel into them as they drop a little. Whenever our threat response gets kicked up, our shoulders start sneaking up to our earlobes. It can be like we're wearing our shoulders as earrings. See if you can bring your scapulae (shoulder blades) down your back and allow your shoulders to rest. Go through these steps as many times as you need to until your shoulders feel completely relaxed.

Now try bringing your gentle attention to your elbows and wrists as they move about. Reach out, push up, turn them this way and that. Bringing awareness to your joints like this fosters proprioception as well as a sense of physical embodiment—my body, my self. Proprioception is the ability to sense stimuli arising within the body regarding position, motion, and equilibrium. Even when a person is blindfolded, they know through proprioception if their arm is above their head or hanging by the side of their body. This exercise of moving our joints with focused awareness enhances this sense and so deepens embodiment. In other words, you feel as if this is your body, your physical home. You can reside here.

You may find this exercise to be highly relaxing. You may also note places of tension in your body here and there that you might not have detected before. This is normal. You're just noticing more because you're giving your body a new type of attention. Whenever you notice tension like this, give that part of your body a little more attention and try to open a space of deeper relaxation. Take as much time with this as you'd like. Try doing it different ways—like starting on the left side of your body and then moving to the right side or beginning the practice with each toe, one by one. All sorts of physical and emotional responses can come up when you do this exercise, and that's okay, too. If old stories or physical symptoms come up in your awareness, notice them and then do your best to stay focused on what's going on in the present moment. This will help build your ability to make a crucial distinction between the past and present, not to mention help you see more clearly how old circumstances influence current experiences.

Hypersensitivity, Signal Cry, and Self-Perpetuating Cycles

Whereas avoidant people have an overabundance of left-brain activity, those of us who are ambivalents experience a surplus of right-brain activity, which can signify an overactivated and hypersensitive attachment system. We might remember the emotionally nuanced past—especially how we felt about it—a lot better than avoidants do, but often do so negatively by dwelling on and replaying past hurts and disappointments over and over again.

At times, our hypersensitivity manifests in strong reactions to the expressions and emotional nuances of others, past or present, as well as an increased anxiety in the face of disconnection or misattunement. Ambivalent people are the most prone to projection, and they can be quick to anger at the smallest slight, actual or imagined. For this reason, there's often a marked absence of ease and relaxation in their intimate relationships. Whether we're talking about ourself in the realms of parenting or romance, this type of hypersensitivity can rob us of critical downtime and actually foster the separation we fear from others. We may unwittingly push away the person we want to love the most.

In some ways, it's as if the ambivalently attached person's signal cry is always on. This is not a trivial reaction. It can't be countered easily with positive thoughts because it's inextricably wired into our sense of survival. So we're trying to untangle that sense of urgency and propensity to experience unsettling threat responses because they feel as if we're actually going to lose the person with whom we're attached—our primary attachment figure. Ambivalently attached people may also get jealous easily. We can go into blind rages if our partner interacts with anyone else in a flirty way because we are particularly wired toward "mate guarding"; we are afraid that we might lose that person at any moment. The threat seems so real that we feel the need for hypervigilance and suspicion.

For all of us, a signal cry sometimes expresses a need for connection. But when that cry is chronically on, the ambivalent person can feel they have to overstate their feelings: if they don't make enough noise, will anyone hear them? Sometimes this comes out in the form of regular cries for attention and other times as pressured word flow (highly intense interactions loaded with excessive and hard-to-follow details), verbal chatter, or habitual complaining. In some cases, people with the ambivalent adaptation are chronically ill or suffer from a myriad of ailments, unconsciously ratcheting up the signal cry through the body in order to attain the connection they long for—especially if that worked in childhood. These overstatements are understandable when you consider that ambivalents have often grown up wondering if their needs are going to be met from moment to moment. Connection was inconsistent and too often interrupted, so instead of being relaxing, the parental connection disturbs affect modulation and autonomic nervous system regulation. This situation is fundamentally confusing and anxiety producing for a child, so it's understandable that, as adults, extreme reactions come up so readily. Ambivalents are very hard to soothe even when their loved one returns.

Unfortunately, our attempts to stabilize personal connections in these ways—hypersensitivity, jealousy, and overstatement—often result in what we fear most. We can unintentionally push people away, which reinforces our fundamental belief that others are just waiting to abandon us. Furthermore, when our own anxiety plays such a major role in our relationships, it can undermine trust and prevent deep connection and growth.

Our great hunger to connect is wrapped up in our belief that such connection is not possible, and our behaviors keep this paradox alive for us. Even if we don't worry about abandonment around every turn in the road (or aren't conscious of doing so), we can project ongoing disappointment onto our relationships, regularly expecting forms of rejection and rewounding to occur at any moment. We expect to be let down or hurt by our partner, even before they do (or don't do) something that might prove emotionally difficult for us. This keeps our sadness and woundedness alive and ensures that we will continue to be easily triggered by relational ups and downs. These are extremely painful cycles to find ourself caught in. The good news is that there are multiple ways to help ourself and those around us to get out of loops like these in order to escape this cyclical suffering.

Need for Reassurance

The couple, Henry and Georgia, that I mentioned at the beginning of this chapter were able to articulate their issues in counseling and find a solution that spoke directly to Georgia's anxious need for reassurance and also helped Henry approach her from his distancing avoidant stance.[4] Gradually, Georgia began to feel more reassured and less anxious, which allowed her to trust the relationship more. As her attachment system began to take the nourishment in, it was easier for her to greet Henry at the door in a more regulated way.

Reassurance is important for all of us, but especially for those of us who are ambivalently attached. Keep this in mind if you have an important person in your life who lives with the ambivalent adaptation. Reassurance and staying in regular contact—through email, texts, or phone calls—calms an overactivated attachment system like nothing else. This doesn't mean that you have to constantly reassure your ambivalent partner for the rest of your life. Just as in the example of Georgia and Henry, when an ambivalent person feels reassured, they experience more stability—primarily by getting to experience object permanence and object constancy in a way they were unable to in childhood. This allows them to relax in the direction of secure attachment, which benefits everyone in the relational field. Ambivalents obviously want a relationship, and generally speaking it is easier for them to maintain one, especially with a secure partner who is willing to be consistent and reassuring. And if you yourself feel aligned with ambivalent attachment, try the following simple practice to offer deep reassurance to yourself.

EXERCISE   My Consistent and Predictable People

Start by grounding yourself in a comfortable spot. Feel your feet as you press them into the floor and pay attention to all the sensations that arise as you sit in your chair. Drop into your seat, relax, and let the chair support you. You don't have to do anything else—the floor supports your feet, and the chair keeps you upright. Relax into these sensations for a couple of minutes.

Now scan your relationship history for people who've had a significant influence on you—family, friends, mentors, or teachers. Pay particular attention to anyone who's been there for you over the years in a reliable way. I'm not talking about people who have been perfect, just those who have been somewhat reliable. Find someone with whom you feel a level of trust, even if you haven't heard from them in years. This is a person that as soon as you see their face or hear their voice, you feel a sense of undisturbed connection—you know this person supports you and always will. You never have to try to be more than what you are with this person. They're present for you, they love you, and they believe in you.

If you haven't had people in your life fill this role particularly well, start with what you have and choose the one who comes closest. Alternatively, you can design the ideal consistent and reliable person to use in this exercise. Or if you know several people who fit this description, start with just one of them. You can add more along the way if you'd like.

How do you feel when you imagine this person? What happens in your body? Notice any signs of relaxation or regulation. Maybe you feel a bit warmer than you did before, or perhaps you are breathing more deeply and evenly. What do your shoulders feel like? Note any changes around your heart and in the muscles of your face. Pay close attention to which part of your body relaxes the most. The attachment system is held in the body, so we want to note what happens here. You can also pay attention to anything that comes up emotionally. Maybe it's a love for this person, or perhaps you feel safe and contained, or maybe you note a sweet sadness. As best you can, feel all aspects of what it's like to be in the presence of this consistent, reliable, loving person.

This exercise may bring up memories of a person you've lost. If so, give yourself time to grieve—and realize that grieving shows that you have the capacity to love and connect deeply.

After you finish this exercise, write a few notes about who came up in this practice and what happened as you imagined that person. Describe what occurred in your internal movie. Maybe you felt different responses to people as you scanned through your relationships. In the future, try this exercise with someone else in mind and see what comes up for you.

"Yes, But . . . "

Years ago I worked with a Dutch woman, Kim, at one of my attachment recovery workshops. She said, "I have this pattern in which I seem to always fall in love with emotionally or physically unavailable men, such as in long-distance romances. The relationships all end about two years in. These guys just can't love me, connect with me, or be present for me enough of the time." As I listened, I tried to set aside the fact that what Kim said might be 100% accurate—that she happened to have had a string of emotionally or otherwise unavailable partners in her life. Instead, I did my best to listen with an ear attuned to early attachment difficulty.

Her current partner, Johan, was a businessman who traveled a lot, and Kim also felt that he was unavailable—just as all her previous boyfriends had been. I asked her what Johan did to show his support and care of her. "Nothing, really," she replied. "He's like the others—always busy doing something else and not very available." But I pushed her a little to more closely examine his behavior because it's a hallmark of ambivalently attached people to dismiss caring behaviors in others. See, if you're a child with unreliable parents, and you take in those rare moments of love and support, you open yourself up to a lot of additional pain when the abandonment happens later. It's just too risky. You can't turn the signal cry off because your survival is at stake. Of course, when you're an adult, this situation has drastically changed, but your attachment system doesn't know this.

Kim looked puzzled. "Well," she began, "he calls me every night to see how my day went. And he wishes me sweet dreams, and actually that feels pretty good." I asked her to feel into her body. How did she feel when she knew it was him calling on the phone? "Warmer, more relaxed in my belly," she replied. She even began to smile a little. I asked her to examine their relationship more. Were there any other caring behaviors she noticed? "When he travels to different countries, he brings me back presents. Special things like jewelry or things he knows I might like. And when he comes back, he often plans a special weekend for us—usually once a month—where we can just be away together in an undistracted way. And we really do connect during those times."

I want to emphasize how shocked Kim looked as she began to acknowledge and list all the caring behaviors Johan had been directing her way. This was totally contrary to her day-to-day experience of him, yet here the evidence was, as clear as day. All she had seen before was his ongoing unavailability—everything that was missing. She was now able to go even deeper in her exploration. "I'm afraid of seeing it," she said. "When I take in this goodness, I get afraid. I just know I'm going to lose it all." This is the dilemma.

For those of us who identify as ambivalents, getting what we long for from others—love, affection, security, and so on—can feel a little like finding ourself in a deliciously comfortable hammock. We really want to relax, but we keep wondering if the damn thing is tied on tight enough. We just know it's going to fall apart at any moment and drop us painfully to the ground. We might be able to briefly recognize the good offered to us in the moment, but we get focused on the future: Will it be there tomorrow? How can we be sure? Essentially, people with this attachment style live with a profound desire for connection, but when we achieve that desire, it's actually difficult for us. We want it, but we don't know how to have it when it comes our way. Our hunger for closeness is matched only by the fear that comes up when we achieve the closeness we've been looking for. As a result, some of us become quite expert at deflecting or minimizing our partner's attempts to show their love for us, or we find ways to create disconnection and distance (arguing, acting defensively, or treating our partners with jealousy and suspicion).

This is the experience of ambivalent attachment that we need to get to the heart of. We need to uncover and unpack these physical and emotional experiences so that we can own our attachment dilemmas. We need to see just how powerful this "Yes, but . . ." response is in our life, and how limiting it can be. Understanding this can help us take in the love and support that are there without endlessly qualifying, diminishing, or negating the goodness already present in our life. It might seem strange that some of us are prone to reject positivity like this. After all, isn't it what we want out of life? But remember just how powerful our physiological patterning is: on an unconscious level, we believe that our survival is at stake, that if we turn our signal cry off, stop talking or stop complaining, we will lose our primary attachment figure, which is very threatening. We need to discover that this is not necessarily the case. As we calm our signal cries, we may be able to be even closer to our partner and actually enjoy the connection and be fulfilled instead of being swept up in our fear of losing it.

GOING FORWARD

I've already offered a couple of exercises to help counter some of the struggles that come with the ambivalent adaptation, but I want to spend the rest of the chapter offering some other ways to steer us toward secure attachment.

SAS #12 Revisited   Noticing Caring Behaviors

Nodding once more to Rick Hanson, all of us can work to stay with positive experiences a little longer than we usually do in order to neurologically repair our tendency to focus on what's negative, dangerous, or depressing in life. Rick Hanson notes that positive experiences flow through the brain like water through a sieve.[5] We have to do what we can to counteract these protective habits in our brain so that we're not always assuming the worst—so that we can receive and enjoy the *best*. This isn't merely a matter of thinking happy thoughts and ignoring our problems and challenges; it's about turning our attention to what's working for us—broadening the aperture to include the good things in life. For people with the ambivalent adaptation, this is especially important to do.

As noted above, those of us who tend toward the ambivalent style often downplay what's working in our relationships—all the good stuff we yearn for but can't seem to find. To counterbalance this tendency, it's important to first begin to *notice* when someone is being loving or kind toward us and then to embody the intention to stay present. Recognize these desirable things when they occur and take a moment to feel the goodness and love in whatever caring words, touch, gestures, looks, acts of kindness, and gifts come your way. Let yourself experiment with how much you can take in and receive from others and lessen your tendency to focus on pain and disappointment. This is more challenging than it sounds, especially when it comes to noticing things that typically escape your field of awareness. It's a matter of paying attention in a new way, but also learning how to gradually trust the goodness in your life.

I became angry one time long ago when my romantic partner said, "You know, every time I tell you how much I love you, you deflect it or start talking about something else. It's like you disconnect from it somehow. It hurts me that you don't take in my love for you." I got mad because I couldn't believe that anyone would think I would do such a thing, but I also didn't want to admit that it was true. After a sleepless night thinking about it, I realized he was right, and it was hard for me to own up to it. Displays of affection had always made me uncomfortable. I had a habit of turning away or changing the conversation because I didn't know what to do with love when it came at me so directly. Isn't that something?

So I made a pact with myself: *Whenever someone shows me love, I'm going to stay present and not disconnect or deflect.* That proved so much more difficult than I ever imagined it would be. It took months of practice before I could stay embodied and connected—to truly feel their embrace, actually listen to their kind words, appreciate their gifts, take in their loving gaze, and feel any of these in a significant, lasting way. Also I became sensitive to the fact that my deflection hurt my partner, and I wanted to receive the gift of his love.

I highly recommend this practice for everyone because I think it offers corrective experiences that will help you tap into the secure attachment network. And I think this is even more true for people with the ambivalent adaptation. First you have to notice the good—a challenge in and of itself—and then let yourself absorb whatever form the love, caring, and appreciation takes. This can be difficult, especially at first, so I suggest taking small steps in the beginning and then building up to taking in more and more. And if it helps, the following exercise provides a more guided way to practice taking in the good.

EXERCISE Receiving 1% More

Find a comfortable seat, feel the sensations in your feet, relax your body, and remember the last time someone approached you in a kind and loving way. This can take many forms: a gentle touch, an act of service, compassionate listening, quality time, or a special gift. Author and healer Gary Chapman has done a lot of work in this arena, and I recommend anything he's written regarding the five love languages. How do you recognize love when it comes your way? What do you value most? How do you show your love? Is it affirmative feedback, physical contact, helpful actions, presence (as in sharing quality time), or giving presents?[6] Do your best to identify which love language you speak and respond to most fluently.

Now consider that how the people in your life express their love might be quite different from how you prefer to give and receive love. I really like affirming words, for example, but my father never told me he loved me until the very end of his life. He did, however, fix my bicycle and lock the doors at night to keep us safe, and he made sure that everything around the house worked. That's how he showed his love—through action—even though it might not have been evident to me at the time. This distinction can be difficult to wrap our head around at first. Just begin by considering that your love language and that of your partner might be quite different. It might be a simple matter of our missing something that seems obvious to the other person involved.

Do your best to broaden your receptivity to love; cast the net wider. What does your loved one offer you that maybe you haven't fully recognized? Note the full range of their caring behaviors. How do they express their love? As things begin to occur to you—maybe even for the first time—what happens when you acknowledge these caring behaviors? How do you feel in your body when you recognize that your partner has their own individual way of showing their love and support? Don't throw out the gift just because the packaging seems off to you. See what it's like to show your caring in a variety of ways and experiment with accepting love and kindness in however it arrives on your doorstep. This perspective only increases the abundance. As the Italians say, *Abbondanza!*

Notice any instances of "Yes, but . . ." that come up, because they will. Maybe your partner carved out some special time to spend with you, but they didn't listen well enough when you were together. Or perhaps they brought you flowers, but not your favorite kind. Or they paid you a compliment, but something about it didn't feel quite right. If you're a person with ambivalent attachment, you can expect these thoughts to come up. Whenever they do, don't swat them down, but treat them with compassion. Become curious about them and be gentle with yourself. We have this idea that receiving love is supposed to be easy, but for some of us, it can be quite difficult and problematic.

What happens when you open up to all of this goodness, if only a little? Don't overload yourself with torrents of loving gestures, kind words, and affectionate touch—just let in 1% more, one small step at a time. In this way, you can enact tiny shifts and not face the challenge of an immediate monumental change. If you can let in 1% more, what does that feel like? And if that's okay, can you let in another 1% more? If so, keep going at your own pace. Your 1% can eventually build to 5%, and 5% becomes 10% before you know it. Take this exercise slowly, moving 1% at a time, and repeat these steps as often as you'd like. Over time, you'll notice that your capacity to stay present in the face of love grows and grows.

As Kim practiced receiving 1% more and released her fear about losing Johan, her belly relaxed and her heart opened up and she could feel love and appreciation for Johan. She could allow the experience of satisfaction and fulfillment. Instead of wanting to break up with him, she wanted to go home and jump into his arms. As Kim left, she said, "Johan is going to be so happy I had this session!" Now she could see and feel his love and caring behaviors.

Self-Soothing and Relational Space

As I mentioned before, ambivalent people often ask for a significant amount of time and energy from their loved ones because they feel that their needs are primarily met through other people. As ambivalents, we didn't learn to adequately regulate on our own as children, so we're constantly looking to others for satisfaction and safety. Of course, from a partner's perspective, this can be challenging, and the tendency to ask for more and more can put undue strain on any relationship. There's nothing wrong with leaning in to our relationships and asking for support and love, of course, and I don't want to discourage anyone from doing so. It's just that we want to learn how to achieve the optimal balance between co-regulation and self-regulation.

Find ways to practice self-soothing behaviors. I'm not talking about doing so in response to every troubling event that comes up, however, because regulating with others is normal and desirable. Secure attachment naturally involves others! I'm referring to expanding your innate ability to take care of yourself a little better when you become anxious or afraid, particularly in the face of relational misattunements, perceived or actual. What helps you relax that doesn't involve anyone else? Try listening to soothing music or dancing by yourself. Take a walk in the forest, practice one of the exercises in this book (especially the "Physical Grounding" exercise we did earlier in this chapter), meditate, do yoga, go for a run, or simply take a few deep, nourishing breaths.

It can also be self-soothing to reflect mindfully on whatever strong feelings get kicked up in interpersonal interactions. As we stay with them, they may complete, transform, and heal us. This only works with the proper dose of compassion. Recall that we suffered a lot of pain as a child, and much of that includes formative trauma that we can't even remember. For this reason, we are sometimes susceptible to exaggerated feelings and responses, and we are capable as adults of looking at that tendency with clarity and kindness. Being able to engage the prefrontal cortex in this way activates the secure attachment network, which in itself is a wonderful form of self-regulation.

As a bonus, when you are able to soothe yourself better, your loved ones won't feel as responsible for your emotions. As you move your co-regulational habits and self-soothing behaviors more into balance, it will increase the healthy space in your relationships. In turn, you and your partner will enjoy your connection with greater ease.

Distinguishing the Self and Restoring Connection

Admittedly, giving loved ones more space and learning how to soothe ourself can be particularly challenging for those of us with ambivalent attachment, so I want to offer another angle here. Consider this: People with ambivalent attachment are uniquely gifted. We walk through the world with incredible sensitivity and capacity. We are able to resonate with others deeply, know them well (sometimes picking up on what they need even before they do), and focus on them in unique ways. I want to recognize how precious that gift is while at the same time help you foster the ability to connect with yourself, because living with a self-connection deficit means that we will struggle in life far more than is good for us. It's too painful to be out-of-touch with ourself, especially when the techniques for living otherwise are readily at hand.

One way to try this out is by looking at the *you* of *you*. What does that mean? Well, taking myself as an example, what do I mean when I refer to myself? Who is the *Diane* of *Diane-ness?* I know it sounds a little silly (and it is), but what I'm trying to get at is that special sense of *you*—your own individual experience in the present moment. What emotions are you feeling? What's going on in your body? What thoughts are popping up and connecting and dissolving? Apply some kind attention and take a look at your unique experience as it comes and goes, moment by moment. Dan Siegel has an exercise I recommend called the "Wheel of Awareness" in which he also points out the importance of learning how to connect with ourself authentically and practice shifting our awareness to different modes of perception.[7]

Ambivalent people have a tremendous amount to gain from restoring a sense of self-connection. Among other things, it allows us to develop more relational sensitivity, true mutuality, and resiliency. As I've mentioned before, being more in touch with ourself improves our ability to understand and relate to others; it also enables us to attune to the dynamic field that arises when we're in relationship with another person.

It can sometimes be difficult for those of us with the ambivalent adaptation to attune to ourself while in the presence of others. This can be confusing, but it isn't necessarily an obstacle. If this struggle sounds familiar to you, try the following exercise. It's meant to help you experience healthy boundaries and maintain self-connection while in the presence of others.

EXERCISE Being With

Begin by taking a few deep breaths and getting in touch with whatever physical sensations come up. Pay attention to any spots of discomfort, physical contact with the ground or chair, muscular tension, or relaxation. If it helps, you can revisit the "Physical Grounding" exercise that appears earlier in this chapter before diving into the rest of this practice. Whatever you do, simply relax into your own physical awareness for a minute or so.

Some people like to keep their eyes closed for the next part of this exercise, which entails imagining that there's someone sitting across from you. It doesn't really matter who it is—your partner, your child, your friend, a stranger, or your dog. If you are doing this practice in a session with a therapist, it could be your therapist. If someone is physically present in front of you, try keeping your eyes open just enough to see their shoes—just so you remember that someone else is actually there with you.

As you imagine this person in front of you, notice what happens in your awareness. Track what occurs when you include someone else in your experience. We began this exercise with just you and your sensations, but now there's someone else right there. What happens? Does your awareness jump to the other person and stay predominantly there? Do you lose any connection with yourself, particularly with your physical sensations? If so, come back to your own body by wiggling your toes and noting the feelings you identified at the beginning of this exercise. The brain gets 80% of its information from the body, so any time we move—especially at our joints—we flood our brain with physical awareness. If it helps you connect to yourself, get up and walk around a bit before you sit back down. Get to a point where you reconnect to your essential *you-ness*, take a few breaths, and imagine the person sitting across from you again.

Once you feel better able to tune in to yourself while simultaneously imagining another person in front of you, see if you can move your awareness from your own body to include their physical presence. What happens? Do you lose any connection to yourself or your physical sensations? If so, feel into your body, shift your focus back solely to yourself, and try again. Work toward establishing a connection to yourself *and* the other person—that is, not *either* yourself *or* the other person, but *both* of you at the same time.

Play with your awareness. Move it around to scan your body and then back to the other person. Expand your awareness in such a way that encompasses both of you—the entire relational field. If at any time you feel disconnected from yourself, gently reground and try again. Don't leave yourself out! Like most things, practice will enable you to improve this capacity—awareness of self, awareness of other people, awareness of the entire relational field. This ability signifies that the secure attachment system is online and fully operational.

One of the good things about this exercise is that you can perform it in real time: whenever you find yourself getting lost in the experience of another person, let that be a warning bell or red flag to come back to yourself. Take a little time-out to reconnect to your own experience and remember that it's possible to have a thorough awareness of yourself and the other person at the same time.

The main thing that I want you to remember is that a major component of healing for ambivalent people involves reconnecting to themselves in one way or another. The exclusion of others is not the goal, but in the beginning, you might need to focus on yourself before gradually (as in the previous exercise) including other people. For those of us who are ambivalently attached, it's important to correct any loss-of-self experiences we have. As we learn invaluable tools to self-soothe as well as reach out to others for comfort and support, we begin to notice caring behaviors and receive love that is already there to feel satisfaction and fulfillment. We reduce complaining and practice receiving as we ask for our needs more clearly and directly. We find pleasure in our alone time as well as in connection and can transition back and forth with more ease.

Lovingkindness

The behaviors and experiences we hold in our body come from a long time ago. We learned and embodied particular action sequences before our mind was capable of forming a story about our experience, and really, we did the best we could with what we had. So, in all things, take it easy on yourself. Do your best to hold yourself with compassion. This work isn't about heaping more judgment on ourself, but about taking a closer look at what serves us in the present moment and what doesn't. It's about regaining our openness, our resourcefulness, and crossing the bridge to secure attachment.

When we own our attachment style with compassion, we gain access to options that most of us thought impossible. If you identify with ambivalent attachment, try becoming a little more curious about relational discomfort when it comes up, as it inevitably will. If you tend to blame others or hold them responsible for your emotions, see if you can gently come back to your own body with kind attention and attune to your emotional self. You deserve it. The ability to move through and dissipate discomfort is right there for you to access on your own. Remember, it's your birthright. And claiming that natural ability will lead to a much more fulfilling experience of yourself and whatever relationships you choose to engage in.

QUESTIONS TO ASSESS
FOR AMBIVALENT ATTACHMENT

- Do you often find yourself yearning for people who feel unavailable to you?

- Do you sometimes apologize for things you haven't done, simply because you fear upsetting or losing the other person?

- Do you lose yourself or become merged in relationships? Are you overfocused on others? Underfocused on yourself?

- Does your partner sometimes describe you as needy or clingy?

- Is it difficult to say no to others? Do you have trouble maintaining healthy boundaries?

- Do you often second-guess yourself or lack confidence in your words or actions?

- Do you feel like you typically give more than you receive in relationships? If so, do you often end up feeling resentful toward the other person, even to the point of holding a grudge?

- When a partner expresses love and appreciation, how difficult is it for you to recognize and deeply feel their caring behaviors?

- How difficult is it for you to be alone?

- When you are alone, do you regularly feel abandoned, stressed out, hurt, or angry?

- Do you yearn for connection yet feel afraid of losing whatever relationship you're in?

- After time away from your partner (say, after a vacation or business trip), do you regularly feel upset or pick fights with your partner?

- Do you feel you can easily attune to others' feelings, wants, and needs?

- Do you feel you need others to calm you down, and do you find it difficult to self-soothe?

- Do you often find yourself living in the past, not able to forgive or forget old injuries?

- Do you find yourself complaining a lot and overlooking or dismissing caring behaviors from your loved ones?

4

DISORGANIZED ATTACHMENT

The disorganized style is the most complex of all because it's an entangled attachment system—it's entangled with our instinct to survive due to excessive fear in our original attachment relationship—and it hasn't been studied or written about as much as the other attachment styles. It's complicated, too, because this style doesn't present reliable behavioral or experiential patterns to track; it's irregular and marked by sudden shifts, and that can make it tricky to understand and work with.

The disorganized pattern develops in response to having a parent or caregiver who was frightening too much of the time. A parent may actually be afraid of their children or still be dealing with unresolved trauma and living in fear, anger, or dissociation themselves. Birth trauma, overwhelming life events, or serious medical procedures that interrupt the connection between parent and child early on can also be contributing factors that result in our feeling that relationships are dangerous.

When reacting to the fear, threat, and dysregulation in this pattern, children may naturally act out the distress they cannot contain, often causing them to be seen as a "problem child." They are then punished for their dysregulation, which only exacerbates the difficulty. In the extreme, this pattern may contribute to addiction, psychiatric conditions, personality disorders, or criminal behaviors.

When parents are scared and fail to regulate their own distress, they cannot calm their child's distress either. The child spends way too much time in overarousal, with high levels of activation in the energy-expending sympathetic nervous system (the fight-or-flight state) or overactivation in the energy-conserving parasympathetic (shutdown or dissociative) state. The child's range of resiliency or window of tolerance shrinks, so it is much easier to be triggered and feel off balance. The child has trouble with self-regulation or self-soothing and cannot regulate well with others either. Any emotion may lead to acting out, or there can be a chronic disengagement. The brain and body become sluggish, which can result in a lack of motivation, disconnection or spacing out, poor impulse control, low comprehension, and underperformance in school.

Kids may also have trouble socially—for example, misreading friendly cues as aggressive due to threat activation—and find friendships hard to come by, so the connections they need for healing are pushed further and further away. The child is often identified as the problem, when it's the dynamics at home that may need the most attention. People with the benefits of secure attachment may have difficulty understanding the chronic stress that insecurely attached folks encounter, especially the severe distress those with the disorganized attachment adaptation live with daily, often with very little relief.

In some ways, disorganized attachment is a combination of the avoidant and ambivalent adaptations, but it is mixed with fear-induced survival defenses switched on to deal with ever-looming threat. Some of us with disorganized attachment lean to the avoidant side and are more shut down and disconnected. Others lean to the ambivalent end of the disorganized spectrum, living in high anxiety, panicky, or rageful states. Some oscillate between both high anxiety and depressive states. There are also those of us who are only "situationally" disorganized, meaning this style only arises in response to particular triggers such as yelling or seeing violence on TV. Let's briefly review the attachment styles we've already covered to see if we can get our footing before moving forward to explore the disorganized attachment style—what it looks like, how it might arise in the first place, and some ways we can repair for ourself and others.

Children who grow up securely attached are able to regulate their nervous system with the help of their parents or other caregivers. Most often they're supported, they feel loved, they recover from being upset more quickly, and as a result, they're able to build on functioning co-regulation to develop effective self-regulation as well. Because they also find it easy to ask for help or seek out support when troubled or threatened, securely attached people enjoy the safety of their community when needed. We need both types of regulation throughout our entire lifetime—self-regulation and co-regulation—but in normal development, children learn interactive regulation with caregivers before they begin to regulate more on their own. As a result, they have a lot of relational resiliency because these two forms of regulation are appropriately developed, available, and in balance. For this reason, securely attached people enjoy a lot of options for coping with life's inevitable challenges.

This isn't the case for people with the avoidant and ambivalent styles. Neither avoidants nor ambivalents received satisfying or consistent interactive regulation in early life, for various reasons, but the ways they adapted to that deficit as they grew up are different. Avoidant people don't seek to regulate with others because they never had a good experience of that happening in the past. The parent was unavailable or so negative that the child did not experience the needed co-regulation enough to imprint it on their own nervous system. The child loses the sense of other. Avoidant people might appear to be expert self-regulators, but they often regulate alone in a way that is more akin to dissociation. Ambivalent people, on the other hand, are primed to seek co-regulation from others, often to the exclusion of self-regulation, and this type of reaching out can take the form of simply wanting others to take care of them (that is, without much mutual exchange) and the loss of their sense of self. Adapting to the limitations of their parents' caretaking styles, you could say avoidants are under-dependent and ambivalents overly so.

Both of these attachment styles are wired into survival: avoidant people are conditioned to survive by orienting toward themselves and dismissing or not needing others, and ambivalent people, with little self-orientation, are trying to survive by constantly reaching out to others for love and nourishment while disconnecting from the self. Their ongoing struggle to receive kindness may actually push loving behaviors and caring partners away. The challenge for avoidant folks is allowing other people in enough so that they can experience and learn interactive regulation and enjoy the true nourishment that comes from relational connections. And a useful corrective experience for ambivalent people is to learn how to develop their sense of self, self-soothe, and practice truly mutual interactive regulation. They have to cease abandoning themselves so they are there to notice and receive the love they seek. For those of us struggling with the disorganized adaptation, the most important corrective experiences are learning both to self-regulate and to co-regulate to increase our sense of relative safety and find clarity that dispels confusion.

RANGE OF RESILIENCY

Dan Siegel talks about the "window of tolerance"—the optimal zone in which an individual feels neurologically at home.[1] In this zone, we feel alive and receptive but not overly stressed; we can relax, enjoy alertness, and we're not depressed or shut down. Our nervous system is doing its thing—going up sympathetically to enjoy energy and aliveness, and rhythmically shifting to the parasympathetic system to enjoy relaxation, rest, and digestive activity in response. We get energized and activated, and then we shift back into relaxation, just like we're riding up and down on gentle waves. This is another way of describing what it's like to be securely attached: our nervous system is working as it is designed to. But regulated, securely attached people don't have a static window of tolerance; it expands in capacity. Since they are regulating by themselves and with others appropriately, over time they can tolerate higher highs and lower lows without leaving their zone of comfort (which I also like to call the *range of resiliency*).

Those of us with ambivalent attachment more easily leave this ideal range by going up in sympathetic arousal and exiting at the top of that window of tolerance—meaning we experience intense emotional states such as anxiety, panic, anger, and even rage. The attachment system is turned on too much; it's incredibly sensitive and often overreactive to relational misattunements and mistakes, stuck in a fear of impending abandonment and not able to relax in safe contact when it is there.

Avoidant people, on the other hand, are often unknowingly expending a lot of energy to block healthy, natural longings for attachment and may leave the optimal window of tolerance by descending into parasympathetic overactivation, which means lower affect, reduced vitality and interest, and decreased engagement in interpersonal relationships—especially intimate ones. In this way, their attachment system is turned off, deactivated. They disconnect, dissociate.

Remember that avoidant, ambivalent, and disorganized insecure attachments are on a continuum. You can have a slight or strong orientation to one pattern, or you might experience a mix of attachment adaptations depending on the relational environments you are in with different people. You can also live mostly in secure attachment but have certain triggers that shift you temporarily into insecure attachment.

Regardless of whether it's stuck on or off, our attachment system can become dysregulated. Similarly, our nervous system can become dysregulated with too much sympathetic arousal or too much parasympathetic shutdown. And particularly relevant to the disorganized attachment style, under severe stress, our autonomic nervous system can oscillate quickly between these two poles, resulting in extreme temperature fluctuation, appetite dysregulation (undereating or overeating), excessive or extremely minimal sexual interest, possible fainting, and/or a freeze response with immobility.

CONTRIBUTORS TO THE DISORGANIZED ATTACHMENT ADAPTATION

When we look at people with the disorganized attachment style, we may see a complicated situation characterized by an alternation between two extreme states at the opposite ends of the range of resiliency. Those of us with the disorganized adaptation may move between shutting down, turning off our signal cry completely, and switching into hyperarousal and keeping our signal cry on all the time because our attachment system is so entangled with the threat response. It's a decidedly painful experience. Or we can be "disorganized avoidant," where high stress or threat causes fear and withdrawal. One of my clients, Howie, talked about his father who was often quite loud and angry when drinking. Howie particularly remembers being yelled at when he dropped the ball or struck out at his Little League games. Afterward, his dad would disconnect from him by giving him the cold shoulder for a few days. This memory seems to encapsulate many memories of his dad's drunken, angry outbursts. Now loud sounds or voices trigger Howie into a threat response of flight, dissociation, depression, and withdrawal.

Other people might be "disorganized ambivalent," where threat leads toward clinginess, a strong need for reassurance, and excessive worries of abandonment. One of my colleagues, Shelly, kept sending texts to her friend Deidra in Spain with no response for three days. Shelly's texts became more frequent and increasingly demanding. Having been left by her mother at an early age, Shelly became terrified when she lost contact with Deidra. Deidra, not understanding the urgency, eventually replied, telling Shelly to back off, leaving Shelly to reexperience her worst nightmare of rejection. Once they both understood the attachment disturbance Shelly was dealing with, they were able to repair their friendship.

In addition to having a nervous system that may get triggered by real or perceived threat and possibly feels unmanageable much of the time, this chronic dysregulation makes it more difficult for people with the disorganized attachment style to create or sustain stable, intimate relationships in which they feel reasonably safe. Remember that disorganized attachment can be situational, where the distress results from a few specific triggers. Once these triggers are extinguished, a person can recover to secure or avoidant or ambivalent attachment without the threat response also dominating them.

In the "Strange Situation" studies mentioned in chapter two, Mary Ainsworth noticed that some of the children's behaviors didn't fit with the three attachment styles she'd identified (secure, avoidant, and ambivalent). She was the first to focus on this outlying attachment style, which she called "disoriented" (an apt description).[2] In the study, these children might run toward their returning mother, but when they got close, they would suddenly switch tacks and run away, run around in circles, throw themselves to the floor, stand frozen in one spot like a zombie, or hit their mother, as if their threat response were suddenly turned on. Upon further examination, Ainsworth found that this behavior in children was often correlated with early abuse or maltreatment. I also find that some of my clients were raised by parents who didn't necessarily act out in threatening ways but may have suffered unresolved trauma themselves. These parents were often generating a field of fear around themselves that interfered with healthy attachment for the children as well. The children learned to dis-attach.

In secure attachment, children run to their parents whenever they feel upset or endangered. Imagine what happens in the attachment system, then, when the parents themselves are threatening. When caregivers are the source of danger, scared kids have nowhere to turn, and that's terrifying. They're not yet able to regulate themselves, and they can't turn to their parents as a safe haven. That's tragic, and it's also fundamentally confusing on a physiological level. In disorganized attachment, we have two biological instincts at odds with each other: We're oriented toward survival, but we also need our caregivers to help us with that. The attachment system is trying to connect with the parent, but then the survival instinct that fears the parent kicks in and shuts it all down. This sets up an impossible situation for infants because they're completely dependent on their parents for interactive regulation, not to mention their basic safety.

Where else does this happen in nature? Most species that I know of are safe among their own kind. Take rabbits, for example. They're biologically designed to understand the basic fact of predation. They live a dangerous life—constantly trying to avoid becoming lunch for coyotes, owls, dogs, you name it—but when they get back to their burrows, they can relax. They're not afraid of other rabbits; they don't have to be on guard in the company of other rabbits. So there's a basic logic in the rabbit world: there's a clear distinction between predators and same-species, friendly rabbits. They know that the other rabbits aren't going to turn on them; they can rely on being safe in their burrows, cuddling with their families, and generally being cozy. I don't know everything that happens down there, but it's clear that we eventually end up with a lot of extra rabbits as a result.

Unfortunately, we can't always say the same for humans. That distinction in the rabbit world between creatures that are obviously dangerous and creatures that are obviously safe doesn't quite hold up. In the human world, far too many children don't live in safe environments with good enough parenting, with caregivers who are reliable, safe, and protective. And for people with disorganized attachment, the people who were supposed to be protecting us were the ones who hurt us the most, or at least presented some sense of threat much of the time. Unlike rabbits, we have a much more confusing world to contend with.

So the primary contributor to disorganized attachment—as first identified by Mary Ainsworth—is when parents are the source of fear. And, again, this can happen when parents are abusive or when they themselves live with a lot of unresolved trauma. Even if caregivers aren't yelling at their children or hitting them or abusing them in some other way, they can be generating enough fear, anger, or chaos in the environment to cause the child's attachment system to shut down. The following are some other things that foster disorganized attachment:

> **Family Turmoil.** There are a number of factors that can keep a household in chaos on a regular basis—financial difficulties (which can result in poverty, starvation, crime, or untreated illnesses), ongoing addiction, or living in a dangerous environment, to name just a few. When things feel disrupted or unreliable most of the time, children are unable to settle into any sense of security. Living in fear and chaos on a regular basis is not conducive to experiencing secure attachment.

> **Emotional Irregularity.** Another characteristic of parents that can contribute to disorganized attachment is sudden shifts between extreme emotional states. For example, a parent might be happy one moment but then get triggered into a violent rage or descend into uncontrollable sobbing without warning. One of my clients told me that she had

a highly reactive mother who would angrily berate her for minor mishaps, like spilling milk on the table or leaving a jacket on a doorknob, but if a friendly neighbor were to suddenly show up, her mother would immediately shift into her happy face, as if nothing upsetting had been going on just moments before. Understandably, parents who express themselves in such an inconsistent way cause deep confusion in their children.

Confusing Communication. Paradoxical injunctions, double binds, and mixed signals (simultaneous "come here" and "go away" messages) are also fundamentally confusing to children. When parents create unsolvable problems that set kids up to fail, it may affect the children later on. They may not try new things out of fear of failure. They may feel shamed in a way that cuts off their creativity or ability to generate options for solutions to simple or complex problems. They may acquiesce to other people's authority so much that they do not develop awareness of what is right for *them*. They may not acknowledge their own needs, talents, and goals.

Here's an example: My client Frieda had a mother who expected her to clean the house and do other chores on Saturdays. There's nothing wrong with that, of course, but her mother, a perfectionist about cleanliness, found fault in almost everything she did. Either Frieda wasn't doing her chores in the right order, or she wasn't using the right equipment, or she was simply doing the task all wrong. When she'd ask her mother for clarification or guidance—for example, "What do I do first, vacuuming or dusting?"—her mother would never give her a straight answer. Her mother would say, "You've lived here long enough that you should know how to do all this by now." Well, obviously she didn't, because Frieda was told she did it wrong (according to her mother) every week. Later, as an adult, Frieda fretted about her difficulty keeping an orderly home or office. She told me she felt it would never be good enough, so why try? She could organize for a short time and then would give up again. She felt set up to fail.

If you recognize your own upbringing in the preceding paragraphs, it's likely that feelings of threat and danger have played a driving role in your life. Also remember that whatever contributed to the attachment style most prominent in your life today may have occurred before you could form memories or create a story about what was going on. If you have never had much access to a physiological sense of safety, it's sure to be an ongoing, crucial issue. Accordingly, I want to offer a corrective practice now to help you tap into a sense of being protected and held. Believe it or not, it's usually possible to foster and regain a fundamental sense of safety, no matter how tumultuous or painful your childhood was. If that seems far-fetched to you, I invite you to try this exercise and see what happens.

EXERCISE   The Competent Protector

Find a good place to sit. Take a couple of deep breaths, relax, and start to feel your body sitting there. Check out your feet on the floor and your seat on the chair. What do they feel like? Wiggle your toes, get comfortable, and tune in to your bodily sensations. Note how the chair supports you fully: you don't have to do anything right now but sit there, pay attention, and give this exercise a shot.

Now scan your relational history—not for any wounds that might have come up as you read the material in this chapter, but for the opposite. I want you to remember anyone who may have been authentically protective and safe in your life—someone who was there for you, even if temporarily. This is someone who wasn't silent or passive in their care for you, but who took a stand, acted on your behalf, or empowered you in your efforts to protect yourself. This person was "competent" in the sense that they had your back in a way that actually helped you.

Invite the presence of this person into the room now. It doesn't matter who it is: your grandparent, teacher, mentor, friend, dog, or a stranger. Something this person did for you—maybe even on a regular basis—stood out. You know you can rely on them. If you need to retreat to someone safe, they'll be there for you. What's it like to bring this person into your awareness now? Where and how do you notice the sensation or the feeling of support? Do you feel warmer? Does your heart feel more open and expanded? Does your spine lengthen?

A client of mine, Debra, couldn't recall anyone like this in her life, but one time she visited a doctor as a young girl for anxiety symptoms and growing pains, and her mother was with her in the exam room. As the doctor checked her out, he began looking more concerned, and after a while he turned to her mother and said, very directly, "You need to stop hitting this child." At first, Debra thought her mother would attack the doctor, because that's what would have happened to her at home, but her mother simply said, "Oh, okay. I'll stop." That short dialogue between the doctor and her mother freed Debra of much of the physical abuse that had been going on. Doing this exercise helped her recall that doctor and what a profound influence he had on her life through that brief but monumental exchange.

Some of us have never had anyone like this in our life, or at least we can't bring anyone to mind. That's okay, too. There are several ways to bring in a competent protector; you can find one that works for you. You might call to mind a character who stands out for you in literature or film—a warrior archetype of some kind. (Some of my clients have chosen Mel Gibson's character in *Braveheart* or Judd Hirsch's in *Ordinary People*.) Take some time now to think about any representatives of protective energy who come to mind. Feel free to be as creative as you'd like. One client, Carly, chose Wonder Woman for her protector. She even went as far as printing out pictures of Wonder Woman and putting them up in her car and around her house (including on her bathroom mirror) to be reminded of her great power and strength. Carly especially related to Wonder Woman's Lasso of Truth, which she imagined using on her lying abuser. Other clients have used Superman, the Terminator, the Hulk, and Xena the Warrior Princess. Some people use an animal they've known, or they pick one—a lion, bear, or dragon, for example—that conveys a strong, protective presence. Whatever the case, we're looking to contact and relate to whatever warrior archetype feels right for you. We want to tap into and evoke that felt sense of protection in your experience.

If no one or nothing comes up for you—not even fictionally—then feel free to design your own ideal protector from scratch or bring in guardian angels or any other form of spiritual protection that works for you. Whoever (or whatever) your protector is, what qualities do they have? What do they look like? How do they speak? Where do they stand in relation to you—in front, behind, on one side or the other? Is this someone you always want nearby, or maybe they just come exactly when you need them to? Are there more than one of them? A whole army behind you? Two guard dogs in front? Dig in here and imagine your protector as best you can. What shifts in your experience when you open to the felt possibility of having competent protection? Perhaps you can relax a bit, stand taller, feel relief, or even experience grief from not having had enough protection as a child. Take in the experience of protective energy you have access to now as much as you can.

You can also think about any time you have felt and acted protective on someone else's behalf. Some of us who grew up in dangerous households have become quite good at keeping others safe. Not having had that ourself, we became strong protectors for others; that's our alchemical gift to the world. Maybe we do this for our children or our pets or our community or any number of people who are refugees around the world. See if you can relate to manifesting this protector energy. You're the protector. You're not going to let anyone get hurt, feel helpless, or be traumatized in any way. There's something biologically right and necessary about this role. You can't save the world and always protect everyone, unfortunately, but you feel a powerful innate rightness to the desire to keep others safe. What comes up in your body when you tap into the impulse to protect another being, to take care of them when they're distressed or in trouble? How do you feel? Let yourself move into this experience as deeply as you can.

Okay, now imagine that you are protecting your own child. What is it like for your child to know that you're there as a competent protector? You are their sentinel, watching over them. Your child has full confidence that if anything goes wrong, you're going to step in on their behalf with love and protection—no questions asked. What do they feel in their body? How do they experience a deeply felt sense of safety?

You can also try this part of the exercise by imagining yourself as a child witnessing this exchange—that is, between your adult self and your child self. What's it like for the little one inside of you, the part of you who suffered fearful circumstances, to observe your effectiveness as a protective parent? Some people report that they feel the child in them suddenly drop a lot of their habitual hypervigilance; they don't have to scan for danger so much. There's an adult here now who's taking care of all of that, so they can relax a little. See if that comes up for the being you're imagining now. Bring your awareness to this possibility as clearly as you can.

You can also tap into that part of yourself who is watching all of this, seeing you protect others. This part of yourself can get a hint that protectors actually do exist in the world. Let this part of yourself, this observer, consider what it's like to have that sense of safety and protection. What changes in you as you imagine this? Touch base with the younger child self in you. Is there some part of your body that relaxes, that can let go of tension and bracing? Are you able to feel a little more carefree in this moment, imagining this sentinel watching over you? What does your younger self feel when they know that an older version of them is available in this way? Connect the vulnerable child with the protective adult inside you. Let yourself get in touch with any sense of relief or safety that comes up.

When you're engaging any parts of this exercise, pay attention to what happens in your body. You might notice that your shoulders drop a little, or perhaps your skin gets a little warmer. Maybe your breathing is easier and deeper. For a while—even for just a moment—maybe you actually feel safe or at least sense the possibility of protection and safety in your life. When you're ready to conclude this exercise, always orient to your surroundings in some way. If you like to practice with your eyes closed (this helps some people visualize), open them now and look around the room. Notice where you are in this moment in time and space. No matter how you conclude this practice, be sure to get in touch with your body again, particularly where it contacts the chair and floor. Take your time to ground yourself before you go about the rest of your day.

After doing this exercise—or between sessions, if you choose to do this exercise regularly—see if you feel safer in your life generally when you practice having a protector on your side in this way. Some people report feeling more curious, more excited, or more eager to explore the world. However your experience manifests, let yourself settle into an emerging sense of safety and see what happens. Try to embody that sense of safety more and more in your life in whatever way works for you. Over time, you can foster a sense of safety in your daily experience and bring it back to your physiological menu.

Here's an example of how this worked for one of my clients, Jeff. Jeff kept watch over his young nephew, Riley, while Riley was swimming in a pool with a group of rowdy friends. Jeff was "on call" if things got too rough, and Riley, knowing he had great backup, could give himself fully to spirited play. I asked Jeff, who had been beaten down as a child by his violent father, what he imagined Riley felt, knowing he had his uncle as a safety net and protector. Jeff said, "Oh, Riley knows I am totally there for him. He can come to me with anything, and I will go to bat for him. I think with me in the picture, he feels free to be a carefree child most of the time."

I then asked Jeff to imagine that the small boy inside of him could see and take in what a good protector Jeff had become as a caring adult. Jeff was familiar with contacting his younger, frightened self, and he responded, "Yes, he is a bit amazed at how big I am now and sees I do a good job with Riley. Riley is so lucky." I then suggested that Jeff, as the seven-year-old, allow the adult Jeff to come in as a competent protector for himself as a child. As he did this, Jeff swelled with pride and relief. Gentle tears flowed as he took in the calming, supportive energy that he had access to within himself. The wounded child now had Jeff as the adult there with him at age seven to keep him safe. Over time and with more healing, Jeff's child self grew up to merge more into the adult Jeff, with their mutual wounds felt and their capacities expanded and intact.

WHAT DISORGANIZED ATTACHMENT LOOKS LIKE

I once had a client named Ellie who had survived a childhood full of intense domestic violence. As an adult, she experienced a lot of emotional dysregulation and struggled with relationships. As we came to know one another in our first session, I was struck by how many of Ellie's personal stories centered around dangerous situations: whenever Ellie encountered a threat, she moved toward it, walking straight into danger time and time again. She hung out in the most dangerous part of the city as if it were no big deal, and she regularly got involved in abusive relationships. Sadly, when Ellie was a little girl, her relationship to danger wasn't optional. Every day after school, she had to walk into a scary household with a violent father, which meant ignoring her natural threat response on a daily basis.

I felt the first task in therapy was to restructure Ellie's threat response. To help her learn to move away from danger (as opposed to toward it), I asked Ellie to identify the people in her life she felt safe with. She mentioned her friend Paul. I asked her to track in her body how it felt when Paul was around. What happened when she felt his safe, responsive, and relaxed presence? Ellie began to feel warm and relaxed, remembering all of the kindness Paul had extended her way. In doing this, she was able to better distinguish people and situations associated with safety. We then shifted our focus to what she felt in her body in the dangerous part of town, including the malicious ogling, glaring, and shoving she'd experienced from some of the seedy characters there. During our session, Ellie was beginning to develop and identify an appropriate physiological fear response to dangerous situations. We need this kind of threat response signal, of course, in order to move away from dangerous situations or to fight back, if need be. I was feeling pretty good about the session; it seemed like we had accomplished some important healing in that brief time. Ellie could detect danger as separate from her sense of safety again.

But when Ellie came back to therapy the next week, she reported what had happened immediately after she'd left my office the week before. As she approached the elevator, Ellie felt that a man waiting there was scary and potentially dangerous. I asked her what she did. She told me that she got on the elevator with him anyway (just like she had had to go into her home to a violent father as a child). It didn't occur to her to wait for the next elevator or take the stairs or wait in the ladies' room until the man was gone or come back to my office to seek refuge.

None of those options came up in her awareness. Ellie didn't think of any of these things because they weren't actions that fit her original programming. Fortunately, nothing bad happened to her in this encounter, and it gave us some good material for our ongoing work together. It was great that she was able to identify the man as potentially threatening, but now she needed to take the next step—to create options for self-care and to take self-protective action.

I had Ellie walk through different options, feel each of them out, practice them, and embody safer actions until she came to feel that she could make better choices for herself. I don't know if the man Ellie saw was actually dangerous, or if she was simply perceiving him that way due to her history with her aggressive father, but it didn't actually matter; she needed to regain the distinction between safety and threat and also recover her active threat response of fight or flight instead of blindly moving toward danger as she had to do as a child. Eventually, Ellie was able to change her habitual patterns in response to danger and orient toward safety.

I'll dive into other methods for reorienting disorganized adaptations in a little bit. I'm bringing up Ellie here to illustrate just one of the many ways we unconsciously act out childhood scenarios in our adult lives, even when particular behaviors don't serve us. Ellie's formative time living with daily domestic violence modified her threat response to the degree that she was unable to distinguish between threat and safety. This is one of many ways disorganized attachment can show up in our lives as adults. We'll explore other ways the disorganized adaptation can manifest in adulthood in the sections that follow.

Threat Orientation

Our attachment system is designed to thrive in safety. When we experience too much fear growing up, everything can get off-kilter. Ellie's adaptation involved not being able to distinguish between safe and dangerous situations, but a contrasting adaptation is when we live continuously on high alert. We can become overly focused on dealing with threats, real or entirely imaginary. And we can be so centered on coping with danger that it makes it difficult to connect to others and develop rewarding relationships, especially when our threat orientation is coupled with cycles of intense emotion (namely, rage and terror).

Physiologically, when the parts of our brain that are associated with survival are activated in this way, we lose access to other parts of the brain that have to do with connecting to other people. When this happens regularly early in life, our interpersonal skills don't develop as well as they might, and this makes it more difficult to attract and sustain relationships as we mature.

Self-Absorption and Controlling Behaviors

Due to an extreme level of inner strife and chaos, those of us with the disorganized adaptation can be quite self-absorbed. Managing such intensity takes a lot of internal focus, and one way that plays out is in controlling behaviors. I'm referring to going through life feeling the need to manage and supervise all the situations and people we relate with. We often feel the need to have control if we have a history of bad things happening to us when we didn't have it. Controlling behavior gets a bad rap, but it makes a lot of sense when you think about it. When you deal with trauma early in life, you're too little to fight back, and you can't just run off and pick new parents down the street. You're trapped in a situation that's incredibly difficult. So you grow up believing that if you could only control things, you'd be safe. The older you get, and the more agency you have, the more you're able to actually take charge of things. And learning to exercise a high degree of control over others usually also serves to enhance self-absorption.

Unfortunately, this tendency can show up in relationships in unpleasant ways. Holding tightly to a rigid sense of how things are supposed to be in adult relationships invariably causes problems because our partners have their own feelings, ideas, and wounds to contend with. Those of us with the disorganized adaptation can also unconsciously recreate trauma scenarios for ourself and people close to us, which may be another way of controlling connection and the relationship itself. It helps to know where our need for control comes from and to treat ourself as kindly as possible. If you happen to have a person with the disorganized adaptation in your life, perhaps it will help you understand their sometimes difficult behavior if you remember the context it comes from.

Lack of Impulse Control

Interestingly enough, people with disorganized attachment can also move through life with too little control, especially when it comes to their emotions. It can be hard for them to manage their feelings, which leads to a lot of acting out. When taken to the extreme, this can result in harmful situations that damage their connections to others. For example, instead of being assertive in a healthy sense, people with the disorganized style can be overly aggressive, prone to violent outbursts, or chronically angry. I'm not saying this is common, but it's an intriguing counterpoint to people who suffer from the need to control everything in their life, and it illustrates the different ways people leave their range of resiliency or window of tolerance. They can also "escape when there is no escape" by dissociating and disconnecting from pain altogether. Finally, having difficulty managing feelings and reactions speaks to the importance of early interactive regulation, which empowers self-regulation later in life.

Ongoing Sense of Failure

When parents use confusing communication in an ongoing way—and especially when children feel set up to fail—kids can grow up with a lack of self-worth and feel like a failure in the face of life's challenges, both large and small. Disorganized people with these feelings often don't like to try new things because they're convinced they're going to fail at whatever they do. Problems can seem unsolvable to them from the outset. Of course, this can bring us a lot of difficulty later in life because school and work both require us to regularly encounter and solve problems. The physiological component of this symptom is similar to the response to threat: when you're flooded with fear much of the time, it's a lot more difficult to concentrate or to actively deal with problems.

Having access to secure attachment and the accompanying safe haven of a secure relationship isn't just about staying safe all the time, and I don't want to emphasize safety at the expense of growth, risk-taking, and empowerment. However, when we do have such a safe haven, it gives us a strong platform to enjoy more confidence to go out in the world, embody our gifts, and make our particular contributions. Many talents go unexpressed due to overwhelming fear of failure and rejection. Safe havens can enable us to work through our problems and challenges and trade disabling constriction for increasing expansion and empowerment.

Internal Conflict and Confusion

The disorganized adaptation comes with a lot of confusion—cognitive, emotional, and somatic. This makes sense when you consider that the fundamental issue with disorganized attachment is that two major biological drives are in constant conflict. We're instinctually driven to connect with others, but we're also programmed to avoid danger and to survive. When there's excess fear in our original patterning, we can feel that relationships are fundamentally dangerous, and yet we long to connect. Often this shows up in ways that are difficult for us to understand. One minute we feel available for intimacy and connection, and then in the next we feel triggered or terrified that something is going to go horribly wrong. The intimacy itself may trigger the feelings of threat from our original attachment scenario. When this happens, we can get stuck in approach-avoid dynamics that are quite confusing to us and to our partners. As I mentioned earlier, the attachment system is always operating. As we gradually rely on our partners more and they depend on us, we become each other's primary attachment figure and feel more trust about not losing the relationship. As our attachment system recognizes the other person as more permanent, this can connect us to our memories of our other primary attachment figures. Sometimes the beginning of the relationship works well, but with disorganized attachment there can be a trigger for danger when intimacy hits a certain depth. Suddenly these intimacy triggers pop up, and we're frightened of our previously comfy partners. Most of the time, this involves body memories that don't have any particular story attached to them. All of a sudden we feel terrified of someone we also love deeply, and this can be incredibly confusing to everyone involved.

Overwhelm and the Freeze Response

The freeze response is a hallmark of disorganized attachment, but it is also common in people of all attachment styles who have suffered significant trauma. When the attachment system is at odds with our survival instinct, it's a recipe for experiencing a freeze response. You may have heard of the freeze response referred to in different ways: Peter Levine uses the term "tonic immobility,"[3] and Stephen Porges calls it a "dorsal-vagal freeze."[4] In this highly charged condition, part of us wants to move forward, and part of us wants to move away. Imagine trying to drive your car like that! You put one foot on the accelerator and one foot on the brake and what happens? The engine revs and revs, but the car is working against itself, nobody goes anywhere, and you could burn out the engine over time. From the outside, it just looks like somebody is sitting in a car that isn't moving. They might even look relaxed. But when you examine the situation closely, you see that there's an incredible tension created from contrasting impulses. The sympathetic nervous system wants to act strongly and defensively, and the parasympathetic nervous system is trying to put the brakes on. A freeze response might look stationary and passive, but it's a state of incredible arousal. It's an extreme state of being "stuck" that's typically fraught with fear, dissociation, and immobility—even paralysis. In this condition, it isn't uncommon for people to lose their ability to hear or speak (the cranial nerve that activates the voice box and/or the inner ear can actually shut off). At the very least, people who live with this adaptation can have difficulty communicating their distress and staying present when it happens.

For people with disorganized attachment, the freeze response isn't a conscious decision, and it can occur any time we feel overwhelmed. I had a client, Amanda, who suffered countless violent outbursts by her mother as a child. She would freeze in the middle of it all, so much that her sister began calling her "zombie child." When we feel confronted with a threat, we can become immobilized like the proverbial deer in the headlights, which is a serious physiological condition that Stephen Porges connects to our body's biological preparations for death.[5] Needless to say, it isn't ideal to remain in the freeze response for very long. We are designed for an easy flow between sympathetic and parasympathetic nervous system regulation as well as between connection and aloneness related to secure attachment dynamics, but trauma can impede both in serious ways.

COUNTERING DISORGANIZED PATTERNS

The good news is that it's possible to separate the attachment system from the drive to survive. This section will offer you ways to counter disorganized patterns in yourself as well as give you tools to help the important people in your life who might struggle with this attachment adaptation. Additionally, there are a couple more exercises to help you regain an experiential sense of safety and protection. You can learn to relax, teach your attachment system to connect to safe people, and simultaneously protect yourself from threat and danger.

Countering the Freeze Response

When I have a client who experiences a freeze response, the first thing I do is acknowledge that something frightening has happened to push them into such an intense physiological state. From there, I employ various techniques to reduce their arousal and let some mobility return. In the freeze state, an energy conservation state, our bodies reduce the intake of oxygen, which means that we aren't breathing deeply. A person in the freeze state can benefit from taking deep breaths, but it's even better for them to return to a stronger sense of safety, and from there, they naturally resume normal breathing on their own. The freeze response can also be associated with cold sensations, lethargy, depression, and often dissociation. When any of these symptoms occur, it's always a good idea to move the body around. Even the smallest physical movements will help someone come out of the freeze response.

I had a client named Katie with a severe trauma history. One of my first goals in therapy was to help her gain a basic sense of boundaries, so I had her sit on the floor and make an outline around herself—a safe zone—with yarn. It was a good start; Katie began to get a basic sense of protection from this exercise. I wanted to see how she felt when I gently pushed into these boundaries, so we agreed that I would roll a Nerf ball toward her. This might sound unusual, but the tricky thing about working with attachment injuries is that so much of it is unconscious. For that reason, we often need to create situations that allow us to take a look at what's encoded in the body, and then we can work from there.

In this case, I gave Katie a heads-up and slowly rolled this soft ball in her direction. On our first try, Katie panicked and experienced a freeze state in response to this seemingly harmless "violation." That gave us a lot of information about what she had repeatedly experienced in her childhood. She simply had so sense of safety; no one had been there to protect her or assist her in developing a defensive response. So we practiced some physical responses. I suggested that she use her arms and hands to keep the ball out of her safe zone, and Katie was eventually able to practice swatting the ball away when it came near. By trying elementary sensorimotor movements of defense like this, Katie began to feel empowered, and eventually this game became fun for her. This might not seem like a big deal to most people, but for Katie, it was a significant shift away from her habitual response of immobility and dissociation. She moved from passive responses to empowering, active ones. Over time, she was able to have more access to her sympathetic nervous system and take the parasympathetic brakes off, so to speak. Katie was able to learn more and more self-protective, defensive actions, as well as gestures of reaching out to others, so she had a growing inventory of responses other than freezing under stress. As I learned from Peter Levine, working with procedural memory and activating defensive responses is important before attempting to process strong emotional states. Accomplishing this gives a person the support and empowerment needed to deal with their intense emotions.

On the flip side, we sometimes have habitual defensive responses that show up unconsciously in our relationships. I'm talking about actual physical gestures that we're not even aware of. We might want to be close to someone, but all of our physical signals make it look like we want them to go away.

I had another client, James, who was a social worker. He was a family therapist, and he was very good with young children. With adults, James was a bit distant, especially with women, who seemed to scare or mystify him. He had struggled to have intimate relationships in his life, and he was even beginning to wonder if he had any capacity for doing so. He liked watching TV programs that featured romantic relationships, but he'd never really had one himself. So I asked him if there was anyone in his life he trusted. Who had his back? To whom did he feel the most connected? James immediately identified his good friend Ron. They did all sorts of things together and really enjoyed each other's company.

I tried a different ball experiment this time. I took a physio ball—a big exercise ball—and I opened the door to my office. I walked down the hall with this ball and had James imagine that the ball was his friend Ron. I asked James to tell me when it was okay to start rolling the ball toward him and when he needed me to stop. He was instructed to notice what he felt in his body when I gradually brought the ball closer to him. When he was ready, I began slowly rolling it in James's direction, getting only a tiny bit closer with the ball before James arched back in his chair and stuck his arms out stiffly, fingers spread wide, palms flat and held up protectively as if he needed to hold or push someone away.

When I asked James to reflect on this seemingly evident physical response, he had no idea what I was talking about. He was completely unaware of sticking his arms out defensively, which indicates that this protective movement was still in implicit, nonconscious memory. I brought the gesture to his attention, we explored what it meant, and after a while we tried the exercise again, but this time James was determined to watch what he was doing with his body. I slowly brought the ball representing Ron a little closer, about the same distance as before, and again James expressed the same response. This time, however, James was able to notice what he was automatically doing with his arms. He was flabbergasted. "I can see it," James said. "It really does look like I don't want Ron to come any closer to me, but I actually like him and want him near." But his attachment reaction had very little to do with Ron; most likely it came from whatever happened to James in the earliest part of his life.

Then I had James arch his back and hold out his arms defensively to feel what it was like to be in that position. James was able to feel an embodied need for space, so much so that he felt he had to defend himself against intrusion. Notice that we're not talking about uncovering any type of story about what happened, not that we could have uncovered those preverbal experiences anyway. In his case, James had no specific memories he could access related to the threat or intrusion. It was more important for him to identify the feelings themselves and begin to consciously enact a sense of having safe boundaries, restoring his capacity to connect in the now and in the future.

James and I continued to work on various boundary-making physical gestures and verbal expressions—holding his arms out in defense while saying "No" or "Get away"—as well as attachment-inducing gestures, such as opening his arms in a receptive way to invite connection. I had him alternate between the two and get used to what that was like because we need both responses in life: we need those boundary-guarding muscles and words, but we also want to be able to welcome others in. In contrast to Katie, it was mostly this latter movement that James needed to evoke and embody. By doing so, he was able to feel openhearted toward Ron on a physiological level. As a result, James became more welcoming and was able to feel more joy in connecting with Ron and to gradually open the door to enjoying more relationships.

When our attachment patterns are activated, we can do all sorts of unconscious things. It's important to move from defensive responses to welcoming ones so that we can let the people we love in. Of course, we need to develop a clear distinction between what's safe and connective versus what's dangerous and intrusive. We need gestures for both programmed in our body.

I wanted to talk about Katie and James here to give you an idea of some of the ways that I approach this work. I hope these examples will encourage you to engage your own creativity on your unique path to healing. I invite you to develop your own interesting ideas for expanding your sense of safety, as well as innovative ways to help people close to you who have the disorganized attachment style.

Boundary Repair

The work I described with Katie is an example of repairing or rebuilding a person's sense of boundaries. Our skin is a perfect example of what a boundary is supposed to do. There's a clear division of what belongs on the outside of our body and what is supposed to be on the inside, and our skin does a great job with that. But skin isn't a rigid suit of armor; it can let things in and out, if needed. It's just the right sort of permeable, allowing for necessary things like bringing in sunlight for vitamin D or letting perspiration out. And when there's some sort of violation—let's say a cut on one of your fingers—your body jumps into action and protects and repairs itself in all manner of ingenious ways. We follow up with bandages or stitches, if needed, to keep this fundamental boundary intact. It's necessary to do so for healing and for our survival.

We also have energetic boundaries that are equally important in allowing us to survive and thrive in this world, although they're usually not so obvious. They can, however, be obvious when it comes to cultural differences. People in Argentina don't feel physically uncomfortable around others until they get within about two and a half feet, but Romanians have a personal space almost double that distance.[6] It can also be conspicuous when we or someone we know is living with ruptured boundaries, which is a hallmark of disorganized attachment or unresolved trauma in general. People with this attachment style commonly have been wounded or traumatized by other people in their life, typically earlier than memories can track. They've been intruded upon in some crucial way—yelled at, hit, or sexually abused—and rehabilitating these wounds involves lots of boundary repair. Developing a sense of intact boundaries is one of the ways we recognize a sense of safety, and safety is paramount when it comes to connecting to others. When we repair our boundaries after they have been ruptured, it reconnects us to a deep and necessary sense of safety. It's wonderful to have this felt sense that our boundaries are intact and functional. It gives us a type of "energetic skin" that keeps us safe as we explore the world.

I want to offer an exercise now that involves exploring the space around you and feeling what that's like. You'll be using your arms a lot (recall that my work with Katie and James had a lot to do with how they did or did not use their arms), so find a comfortable spot and try it out.

EXERCISE The Protective Sphere

Choose either your right or left arm (just one of them—we'll get to the other arm in a bit) and extend it out in front of you. Hold this arm out as if you're reaching for someone in order to connect with them, or maybe you're receiving a gift from this person. It's a simple gesture that doesn't have to do with any particular person. How does it make you feel? Does it feel okay and safe, or maybe vulnerable and frightening? Now try out the other arm. Reach it out as if you're going to receive friendliness, kindness, or some type of loving connection. What happens in your body when you do that? Now, when you're ready, reach out with both arms. Try it first with your arms wide open and then use a gesture in which your arms are closer together. Notice again what comes up. Do you feel relaxed? Are you braced and tense in your body? Pay attention to whatever comes up.

Because we need to feel connected but still know that we can maintain healthy boundaries, let's try an opposing gesture. Place your right hand out in front of you as if to defend yourself. This gesture may communicate a sense of "No," "Back off," or "Get away from me." The words may come later. Now let your left hand join in as if you were making an actual boundary in space in front of you. Imagine now that you're in a protective sphere that surrounds your body at arms' length. Feel around the interior of this energetic sphere. These are your energetic boundaries. Let your hands explore this safe space, painting the walls of it with your palms and feeling all the different sides of this protected globe around you—above, below, in front, and behind. Turn around slowly so that you can feel on all sides of your sphere.

Get a sense of what this space is like. How does this feel in your body? Does it feel safer, and if so, where do you notice that? Do you notice any sense of empowerment? Does one direction feel safer than the others? Take a moment to explore the sphere and find out if any direction or vector feels more protected and safer than the others. Feel the edges of that part of the space. Does anyone come to mind when you do this? If you've already done the "Competent Protector" exercise presented earlier in this chapter, try bringing in your personal protector at this point. Imagine them at the edge of your sphere. See if that helps your sphere expand in any way.

Sometimes when people do this exercise, they spontaneously remember boundary ruptures they didn't know about or hadn't thought of in a long time. If this happens with you, know that it's normal and that the experience might call up some strong feelings and protective words. For example, you might find yourself saying things like "Stop" or "Leave me alone" or "Stay away." Any words that come to you are fine. You can say them out loud or imagine your competent protector saying them. Whatever you choose to do, feel what happens in your body and in your sphere of safety. Do you feel stronger, more secure? Does the sphere seem to expand? Are more sections of space around you available to you in a more intact way?

If this exercise is particularly challenging—for example, if it brings up a sense of overwhelm, or the memories of boundary ruptures are overpowering—I recommend trying it with someone you trust. Have them help you in whatever way feels supportive. If nothing else, it might help you maintain your focus just knowing that someone's right there—someone who has your back.

This exercise is intended to help reconnect to a deeply felt sense of safety. It's so important to regain a sense of feeling protected, to actually feel it in your body. This exercise also promotes healthy, intact boundaries. As you become more regulated, you're less likely to get stuck in a threat response, which in turns means that you'll be better able to feel your energetic boundaries.

Helping Others

You may not identify with the disorganized adaptation yourself, but perhaps people close to you live with this attachment style.

Clearly, this book is not intended to serve as an end-all guide to help-ing these people (or anyone else, for that matter), but if you want to promote safety in others, I highly recommend trying out the following habits. (I'll offer more tips that relate to romantic relationships in the next chapter, as well.) And if you're a person of the disorganized style, I hope you'll feel empowered to request the following practices from people you love:

Communicate simply and clearly. As I illustrated at the beginning of this chapter, people with disorganized attachment often grew up in households with confusing mixed messages. For this reason, it's important to be as clear and direct as possible in your speech, especially when it comes to instruction or directions, or when your partner or child seems stuck in indecision or confusion. This occurs most profoundly in the freeze state, when people can have trouble finding the right words, responding at all, or even forming basic thoughts. When this occurs, giving the disorganized person as few options as possible is the best idea. Even in a less charged state, they might have trouble choosing where to go to dinner among a number of favorite restaurants, and under stress, it's best to reduce any options down to two or three, max. Remember also to describe and explain things to children using age-appropriate concepts and language.

Be mindful of your tone of voice. How we use our voice—especially the prosody, or tone of voice—communicates safety or danger to others. A melodic voice that employs fluid modulation and intonation fosters a sense of safety, whereas a monotone or robotic voice comes across as cold, uncaring, and in some case, threatening. We often use a more musical tone of voice with babies and animals, our voice going up and down with affection in an exaggerated, singsong way. I'm not suggesting going around using the same type of voice with adults, but modulating your tone will certainly help when you're speaking with others.

Think about how people's voices change when they're angry or feel endangered; that's an evolutionary cue to the community that something's wrong. When danger occurs, we are biologically and evolutionarily designed to shift our tone to alert the tribe. Women's voices tend to become high-pitched and shrill, while men lower their tone and get louder, producing a booming voice. It immediately signals to other people that there is danger, that they should stop what they are doing and prepare to defend themselves. But when our voice does this under stress during a discussion or conflict with our partner—a relatively safe person (hopefully) whom we love—it can easily trigger their threat response, shifting them toward fighting or wanting to escape. So if you're interested in reconciliation and a positive result for your relationship, it will benefit you to be mindful of how you use your voice. Practicing a calming, soothing, and well-modulated voice will reduce a sense of threat in your partner when you are trying to work out intimacy issues or relationship concerns. Shrill or booming, threat-stimulating voices will trigger our amygdala, or reptilian brain, that's engaged in promoting survival responses, making our partner appear as an enemy rather than as our beloved.

Practice safe touch. Using touch in a way that's loving and conscious of another person's boundaries also creates a feeling of safety. Physical touch amplifies anything we might be expressing verbally. In *Snap: Making the Most of First Impressions, Body Language, and Charisma*, Patti Wood says that we communicate regulation through regulated touch. That is, when we are regulated in our own body, we can convey physiological regulation even with a handshake. The key is to be centered and grounded in your own nervous system—within your own range of resiliency—before you employ touch in this way. Wood asserts that a simple, regulated handshake can offer more regulation than three hours of affirming, empowered conversation.[7] Safe touch may help you and your partner regulate each other. Be mindful, however, that if your dysregulation is severe, it might be too much to touch another without dysregulating them. The chemistry or energy of your skin on theirs is communicated in a tangible way, so keep in mind the importance of taking time to establish your own regulation first if you can manage it. Think about how regulating hugs are when the other person is calm, loving, and safe. I'm not talking about those quick, pat-you-on-the-back kind of hugs, but the ones that involve bellies touching one another in a full-contact embrace. Try it with someone you feel close to. You can feel each other's bodies regulating from this type of contact.

One technique I often use with clients is to begin by simply sitting next to the person. I feel what that's like for a bit—getting a sense of their energy, so to speak—and allow them to get used to me. I ask if it is okay to place one of my palms near their back, between their shoulder blades, starting in their energy field about three or four inches away from their skin, checking in with them to see how they're doing. If that goes well, and they agree, I gently put my hand on their body and find the right amount of pressure—too much or too little can make a big difference. I also ask them to let me know where the best spot on their back is, and I shift my hand in response. By doing so, I am adjusting my contact in attunement with their request, so they have the experience of having their needs met as I convey safety, presence, and care. For ongoing support, we can teach our partners or family members to do this, too.

Look at others (and use facial expressions) with kindness. How we use our face when we express ourself can also communicate a sense of safety to our partner. The eyes are of particular importance. Remember the beam gleam, that safe attachment gaze I talked about in the first chapter? It involves a lot of eye contact, of course, but also a look that expresses appreciation, love, and a sense that the other person is special. As I mentioned, it's important to invite this type of connection only when the person is available for it and not when they are dealing with shame signaled by gaze aversion. Often their shame needs to be processed a bit before you can establish a nourishing connection with an attachment gaze. These nonverbal messages of connection and kindness really do trigger other people's safety response. Think about the difference in your partner's face when they're angry (scowling, tense) and when they're happy to be with you (smiling, eyes wide and bright). People read your gaze and facial expressions all the time, even if they're not conscious of it.

Now that we've identified some markers of safety and how we can convey them to people with the disorganized adaptation, I want to offer the final exercise of the chapter. If you are someone who identifies with disorganized attachment, I recommend reading through these instructions once before trying the practice. If you think it might be too much for you, feel free to skip it and come back when you feel more resourced. Engage the support of a friend, partner, or trained therapist as you wish. Again, it's important to not push yourself too much and to practice self-compassion whenever possible.

EXERCISE The Attachment Ally Oasis

An "attachment ally oasis" is a place where everyone is reasonably safe, where we feel that we can connect to those around us with relative ease and comfort. Even if we can't populate an island or oasis with select people in real life (if only we could!), this exercise offers a wonderful resource for connecting to your secure attachment network, utilizing the power of your imagination to benefit your nervous system.

Begin by thinking about all the people in your life who feel safe. These people are your allies; they wish you well and have your best interests at heart. These could be people you have known for a long time or strangers you've encountered at some point in your life. Make a note of everyone who comes to mind and picture them all around you—to the left, right, front, and back of you. This is how you build your oasis of allies, but you also need a specific location to put everyone so that you can orient to it. Choose a location and imagine it in as much detail as you can. One of my clients, Connie, saw all of her friendly allies relaxing around her on a floating dock, far away from any disturbances. As we later began to process painful memories, she could shift her attention to the dock full of friends for relief and regulation. Another client, Ken, felt very supported imagining his two dogs flanking him on both sides.

The people you have gathered represent all kinds of wonderful things—safety, presence, empowerment, protection, playfulness, acceptance, and belonging. Take a moment now to feel what it's like to know they are there. What happens in your body? You may find yourself getting warmer, feeling more openhearted, becoming more resourced and resilient, or simply smiling and enjoying the connection to your allies. Take your time with this and feel all the powerful sensations that come up.

Now that you have access to this wonderful oasis with these supportive people, let's try something new and perhaps a bit scary. I want you to remember your caregivers, the people who raised you who had less-than-ideal behaviors or responses to you growing up. Remember that at any time throughout this exercise, you can shift your attention to your ally oasis with all of your support. Perhaps you focus on your father. (You can adjust this example to fit your particular circumstances.) He might have loved you in his own way, but let's say he had a tendency to yell at you when angry. Part of our goal here is to separate those two things from one another.

The loving part of your father is fine, of course; that part is not likely to cause you any problems. But we're going to get some distance from the yelling aspect of your father and place that behavior as far away from you as possible, or at least as far away as your body wants it to be. So whatever your version of this is—perhaps a yelling mother—create the space you need. How much distance do you want from this person? Some people like to imagine the threatening behavior close enough so that they can keep an eye on it, whereas others choose to put it on the edge of the ever-expanding universe. Feel what's right for you. Locate the person exhibiting their negative behavior there.

When you establish the location and distance, I want you to freeze-frame the person with their harmful behavior there. In this case, you freeze your father yelling. Perhaps you have him in a big block of ice, so you can't hear anything. With this threat frozen, he can't move, but *you* can. Maybe your father has tape over his mouth in this scene you're creating, or perhaps you have an extremely powerful remote-control device that mutes his yelling whenever you want. You can imagine anything you wish to help you feel protected from this trigger. You may want to yell back, "Stop!" Whatever works for you is fine as you initiate and complete self-protective responses. It is okay to enjoy the relief. You are not hurting anyone because this is all imaginary, and it can be very helpful to you to free yourself from fear.

Okay, now that the threat is frozen, what does your body want to do or say in response to the yelling? Or what might you want your competent protector to do or say for you? Where do you want your protector in relation to this frozen threat—in front of you, by your side, standing right behind you? When we are little, we need someone there to stand up for us. We learn how to be self-protective by experiencing someone protecting us. So notice how it makes you feel to see your competent protector supporting you this way. And as my client Julia said, "My own body is my protector!" signaling that at times it feels more empowering to do it ourselves.

Find out what else your body wants to do or say. Do you want to make a boundary with your arms and hands? Do you want to tell your father to be quiet, to stop yelling, to speak in a normal tone of voice? Maybe you want to send him to anger management classes and see him receive the help of a fantastic therapist and resolve the issues that underlie his outbursts. Whatever you want to do is fine. See what comes up. No matter what you or your competent protector says or does, your caregiver is frozen; they can't respond or hurt you in any way.

What happens in your body as you do this? What do you feel when you're "safe enough" in the presence of this threat? Notice the changing dynamic: your caregiver is immobilized, yet you are increasingly powerful. Does your body feel larger somehow or maybe older? Do you feel activated in your limbs, as if you wish to kick or hit back? When we are able to move versus shut down, it can release a lot of pent-up survival energy. Can you feel the previously stuck arousal release and discharge out of your body—perhaps as a rush of heat, sweating, trembling, or shaking? Allow this to happen so this excess energy can discharge out of your body. Maybe something has been stuck in you for a long time, something that can finally now be set free. This is one way to unpack the freeze response you might have experienced as a child and bring some of your appropriate defensive responses online.

As you are working with self-protective responses, check in with your ally team on the oasis anytime you need more support. Enjoy and allow yourself to regulate with the team. As you feel more connected to support and grow stronger and come in contact with your adult resources, you may notice your father shrink in size as you grow taller and that the threat fades more and more over time. Once again, remember that you have access to all of your loving allies. Perhaps you see that they embrace you, give you high fives, and look at you with love and kindness. You are safe with them—appreciated and seen. Feel this support as deeply as you can, and feel free to return to this ally-filled attachment oasis whenever you need to. This is your secure attachment network, and it is always on your side.

Nearing completion of this exercise, one of my clients, Rosa, felt so much safer in her experience of standing up to her raging mother and regaining her strength that she completed the imaginary movie by inviting her mother to sit beside her in reconciliation. She could be close now with no fear. This healing led to her being able to accept her securely attached fiancé and to move ahead with their wedding plans.

I hope this chapter has provided some ways of understanding yourself or people you hold dear. Ideally, you won't feel as unusual or troubled in your relationships, and you can go forward with some new ways to heal and feel less stuck in habitual patterns that may not be serving you or your partner. Remember that you have your memories of what has happened, but as the pain and suffering are felt and integrated in manageable ways, they may cease to be overly disturbing. You are designed to heal—secure attachment is innate. You can draw on this biological wisdom. You can learn to act with secure attachment skills, behaviors, and perspectives, and you can enjoy all that they offer.

Reading this chapter might have brought up a lot for you. If so, please remember to take it easy and try not to be hard on yourself. Disorganized attachment is far more prevalent than you'd expect. Clinical psychologist and author David Wallin has said that many therapists have some form of unresolved disorganized attachment, at least situationally, so if you identify with this attachment style, you're in good company.[8] No matter who you are, disorganized attachment can be complex and quite frustrating for all involved, so take small steps as you move forward, and begin by working with people and situations that feel manageable. Gather people around you who will be true allies and nourish those relationships as best you can. Relying on a safe support system is crucial to learning how to self-regulate better and regain the secure attachment that is your birthright.

You can learn these skills. You can learn to self-regulate and co-regulate. You can learn to feel safe. You can cross the bridge back to secure attachment.

QUESTIONS TO ASSESS
FOR DISORGANIZED ATTACHMENT

- Do you perceive intimate relationships as dangerous?

- Do you sometimes become frozen or immobile in relationship with others—times when you feel you cannot move in any direction whatsoever?

- Do you often struggle with mixed messages from other people (for example, "Come here, go away")?

- Do you sometimes experience an inexplicable fear when you reach a certain level of intimacy with others?

- When others approach you unexpectedly, do you have an exaggerated startle response?

- Have people complained that you are too controlling?

- Do you often expect that the worst will happen in relationships?

- Do you feel close relationships may trigger dysregulation that is difficult to manage?

- Do you struggle to feel safe with your partner, even when a big part of you knows they are trustworthy?

- Do you often disconnect, dissociate, or become confused in relationships?

- When it comes to past relationships, do you have a difficult time remembering them or discussing the feelings you experienced?

- Do you sometimes have substantial memory blocks—periods of time or significant events that you can't remember?

- Do you experience unpredictable sudden shifts of state (for example, switching from joy and happiness to fear and anger)?

- When triggered, do you become stressed or confused by complicated instructions and arrangements?

- Do you sometimes feel set up to fail and unable to solve problems?

- Have you experienced deep longings to connect with others and then inexplicably want to get away from them?

5

ATTACHMENT STYLES AND ROMANTIC PARTNERSHIPS

I want to conclude by looking at how we can use what we know about secure and insecure attachment to better our relationships, specifically our romantic partnerships. I've made occasional suggestions in the preceding chapters, but we're going to really dig in now and look at some different ways of viewing romantic relationships through the attachment lens. I want to acknowledge how much I have learned from Stan Tatkin and Tracey Boldemann-Tatkin, creators of the very effective PACT training programs for professionals. Stan has written excellent books that you can refer to for more information and support. You can find several of his titles in the selected bibliography at the end of this book. This chapter is also deeply influenced by the excellent work of Amir Levine and Rachel Heller, coauthors of *Attached: The New Science of Adult Attachment and How It Can Help You Find — and Keep — Love*. They describe the contributions and challenges of the secure, avoidant, and anxious (ambivalent) attachment styles as well as the relational dynamics between them in a very articulate, compassionate, and clear way.

By now, you're familiar with how trauma can impact relationships, especially when that trauma happens early in life. It's also important to remember that overwhelming life events in adulthood (like my car accident, for example) can trigger strong emotional responses, discon-nection, and a loss of fundamental groundedness. As I mentioned in the introduction, I've come to think that—in addition to "tremendous fear, loss of control, and profound helplessness"—a definition of trauma should include "broken connection." Accordingly, our healing comes in the form of reconnection—to our own body, mind, and spirit, but also to other people (especially those closest to us), the planet we all share, and beyond. We need to regain our sense of dependence, independence, and interdependence as well as discover and experience interconnectedness with all humanity. And because we don't heal in isolation, we *need* other people on this path. In adulthood, this usually involves our romantic partners or closest friends, who become our primary attachment figures.

Ideally, we grow up as (or grow *into*) securely attached people; that's what we're wired for. When things go predominantly right in early childhood, at least most of the time (or enough of the time), we yearn for connection and are receptive to others. We generally expect other people to be accepting, appreciative, nourishing, loving, and responsive. Our formative environment was prosocial, so we're accustomed to expressing our needs and responding to others when they do the same. In adult relationships, we experience well-being and mutuality, safety and trust, presence and protection. When misattunements come up, we notice them, readily resolve conflicts, and initiate or receive repair attempts with empathy and compassion. And although things aren't always easy, we typically don't go through life avoiding connection with other humans, and when we do connect with them, we're not constantly anxious about these relationships. We can relax with others in the relational field and we feel at ease alone as well. We can enjoy co-regulation and self-soothe through self-regulation.

Of course, things aren't always ideal. We've already looked at various factors behind the different insecure attachment styles—avoidant, ambivalent, and disorganized—but it goes beyond what happens just between parents and children. Here are some additional things that contribute to how and why we develop the attachment styles we currently embody:

Relational Stability. Children soak up whatever happens between themselves and their parents, but they're also quite affected by the interactions between their caregivers. If parents aren't loving and supportive toward each other, for example, it will diminish a child's ability to feel securely attached.

Relational Support. The type of environment a child grows up in will have a lot to do with their attachment style. Ideally, the mother has support during her pregnancy and when she's nursing, and both parents enjoy sufficient help—be it from each other, family members, friends, or babysitters.

Medical Procedures. The baby and mother might experience a birth trauma together, or there could be an illness to contend with that may result in attachment interruptions. The child could be born prematurely (needing to stay in an incubator for a period of time) or need a surgery in the early months of life, or a parent could get sick and need to go to the hospital. Unavoidable separations at these inopportune times do occur, and these can affect attachment patterning.

Temperament. So much depends on the way a child is wired before they come into the world. This has to do with genetics (including epigenetics related to intergenerational patterning), of course, and what happens with the mother and baby during pregnancy, but it goes without saying that some children come into the world with an easy temperament, whereas others come with a high arousal level or are just more complex and intense.

Environmental Conditions. Regardless of the quality of parenting they receive, children around the world are born into social conditions—extreme poverty, war, and

cultural oppression of different sorts—that can have
a profound effect on the type of attachment style they
develop. However, keep in mind that severe conditions
do not always result in insecure attachment. Even though
they struggle to survive daily, homeless people often
take care of each other with incredible generosity; lower-
income communities are regularly tightly knit and actively
interdependent; and in times of war, people band together
to survive under terrible circumstances.

Other Relationships and Life Events. We're influenced by
every relationship we have. They help pattern us in one way
or another. If we are secure and marry an abusive partner,
we may lose our secure attachment and move toward the
disorganized adaptation. If we are avoidant or ambivalent
and enjoy the company of a securely attached partner, over
time we may move to secure attachment ourself. It may be
more challenging for those with disorganized adaptation
to shift to secure as quickly, but all attachment styles can
benefit greatly by learning and practicing secure attachment
skills, behaviors, and attitudes. Additionally, each of
us experiences our own unique flow of successes and
challenges in life, and these will in part change how
we experience relationships on an emotional and
physiological level.

Whatever insecure tendencies we have, we come by honestly. We can't
consciously choose to create our original relational template. We don't
elect to embed a certain attachment style in our body or to have
our particular assortment of preverbal implicit memories. We don't
choose to project certain storylines onto others and the world or to
have inflexible ideas about what relationships look like, or should look
like, or how they're going to go. We don't choose these things because
a significant amount of this is formed preverbally, before we have a
mind capable of fashioning narratives or even remembering. We can,
however, choose to do something about it.

I think it's also important to recognize the genius of our attachment adaptations and see the inherent value even in the insecure forms of attachment. There have been times in our evolutionary circumstances when danger was immediate and there were limited resources, so we needed to compete and be incredibly self-reliant and self-protective, or we would have risked death. And there have also been times when we needed to be extremely close to others, attuned to them, and hyperempathic in order to survive.

It's important to recognize the factors behind our attachment adaptations because we don't want to demean ourself or feel trapped or additionally wounded by whatever assessment or label we put on ourself. Remember that these adaptations are just starting points. We're all hardwired for secure attachment, healing, and core intactness, and we can draw on that innate potential to return there, in part by learning secure attachment skills. When our early attachment patterning creates havoc on our adult relationships, it's helpful to remember that we're not stuck or doomed. Once we know what secure attachment is, what it looks and feels like in a relationship, we can practice secure attachment skills, become more vulnerable and trusting, take more risks, and enjoy our relationships far more than we ever thought possible. As we regain our capacity for secure attachment, our ability to receive love and give it grows and grows. We shift from blaming ourselves or our partners toward embodying compassion and understanding of this human journey we call relationship.

SECURELY ATTACHED COUPLES

If you're a securely attached person, you bring a lot of value and capacity into any relationship. Romantically, securely attached people pair up with each other a lot of the time; they're naturally attracted to each other, as if brought together magnetically. And I have to tell you, securely attached or securely skilled couples are a joy to be around. Stan Tatkin talks about the importance of finding "mentor couples"—a term he credits to Marion Solomon.[1] Spending time with these couples is a great way to prime your own sense of secure attachment if you haven't seen it at work much in the relationships of others. The more time you hang around people who are securely attached, the more you're able to learn from them to embody the qualities they manifest in your own relationships. As a starting point to what we're after in this regard, here's a brief rundown of what it looks like when securely attached people choose to partner with one another. Find one or two of these characteristics that call out to you and try them in your own relationship:

Mutual Attraction and Commitment. To start with, these partners are drawn to each other. Their relationship is based on mutual attraction (instead of fear or anxiety), and they both really want to be with the other person. They're invested in each other, as well as the relationship itself, and they commit relatively easily.

Foundational Friendliness and Well-Being. These partners are also great friends. They reciprocate without a lot of effort, and they act generously toward each other. They behave as if they're in a sacred position of being in charge of their partner's well-being, and they depend on their partner to provide that for them, as well. You can turn the term *well-being* around to make a *being well*. Securely attached partners draw from the *well* of the relationship and from each other to enjoy *being* present and affirming.

Attention and Specialness. These partners know that they're special to each other, and they let each other know on a regular basis. They pay attention to each other—putting down their phones and tablets when their partner is talking to them (as Kim John Payne says, "Devices can be divisive"[2])—and they treat each other like royalty. They're consistently responsive to each other's needs, taking delight in helping each other with enthusiasm and love.

Humor and Enjoyment. As you might imagine, securely attached couples have a lot of fun together. They have a good sense of humor and often have wonderful nicknames for each other. You get a sense of ease and lightness when you're around them, and their mutual enjoyment is palpable. They take adventures together and like to share new experiences, which helps maintain their attraction to one another.

Co-regulation. These partners practice excellent self-care, and they also experience each other as regulating. Physically, neurologically, and emotionally, these couples know how to calm high arousal states and energize depressive or lethargic states for and with each other on a regular basis. They soothe each other easily, and they know without a doubt that they can go to each other in times of need. Anything that arises in the relationship is held in a safe, resilient, and regulated container.

Security and Risk-Taking. Feeling secure in their connection and intimacy, these couples gain more confidence to assert themselves with each other and in the world. They can explore their lives with openness and curiosity, and they feel safe enough back home to really get out there, take chances, open themselves up to new life experiences, and offer their gifts to the world. This sounds paradoxical, but it makes sense when you think about it. The more safety we experience in our relationships, the more confident we feel in ourself, and that empowers us to develop more autonomy. Amir Levine emphasizes that without a secure base, we can't contribute to the world in quite the same way because we can't afford to take risks.[3] A lot of talent goes unused and wasted out of fear of rejection or lack of support. In a securely attached partnership, we know that the other person has our back, and this opens up the world to us in all kinds of ways. They may take risks that can enhance intimacy with each other within the relationship as well.

Together and Apart. These partners transition easily between being connected and being autonomous. They're comfortable being together or apart, and it's even easy for them to do both at the same time (say, doing different activities while occupying the same room in the house in silence). Their relational field allows a lot of flexibility and movement, and when they're with other people, they're sure to honor agreed-upon boundaries of the relationship and respect each other's privacy.

Verbal Communication. These partners know what's going on with each other. Stan Tatkin frequently says, "Your partner is your go-to person—you go to them first with any significant news or happenings in your life."[4] Securely attached partners talk, they're transparent, they keep each other updated, and they share important information with each other first. They tell each other their worries, disappointments, losses, victories, celebrations, and all sorts of other things, avoiding secrets and little deceptions (even white lies). They use affirming words and say "I love you" frequently, they text one another, and they call each other when apart. Stan says these couples stay "tethered." In one way or another, they find a way to emphasize connection and be there for the other person. They listen reflectively and ask clarifying questions, which promotes contingency and furthers connection, and they are comfortable expressing their feelings and needs.

Nonverbal Communication. Stan Tatkin notes that you can tell when couples are in a secure groove because they practice safe, affectionate touch (lots of hand-holding and hugging), groom each other (for example, picking lint or loose hair off the other's shoulder), and exhibit matching behaviors (crossing their legs in tandem while sitting across from each other, tilting their heads in the same direction, and the like).[5] They communicate their love for each other with kind eyes, their faces are responsive and expressive, and they use a melodic tone of voice when speaking to one another. As I've noted before, all of this communicates safety and calms the amygdala so that connection comes more easily.

Conflict Resolution. I don't want to give the idea that everything is always perfect for securely attached couples. Problems come up—that's just how life is—but when they do, these partners willingly discuss their problems and resolve issues without a lot of difficulty, and they do so in a way that fosters further closeness. Whereas avoidant people tend to shut down and distance themselves; ambivalents may devolve into complaining, loss of self, and controlling caretaking; and disorganized people may get confused, dissociate, or freeze; securely attached people usually move toward one another when conflicts arise. They might argue plenty, but they don't attack, blame, or shame each other; threaten to leave; or seek to destroy the other person. They're generally accepting and open to understanding one another, and their perspectives and behaviors aren't rigid: they can change for the sake of the relationship, when needed, and without abandoning themselves. Stan Tatkin gives excellent advice that you can try out yourself, which is to keep your fights short. No matter what happens, take a break after fifteen minutes or so.[6] This will prevent your brain from encoding the disconnection into your long-term memory, avoiding the risk that these mostly negative experiences encode in a way that your partner becomes seen as the enemy instead of your loved one.

Securely attached couples naturally work to stay connected, even in times of intense disagreement. Doing so gives them a sense of unflappability. They know that conflicts aren't that big of a deal, and they feel empowered that the relationship is oriented toward mutual benefit and togetherness. They believe in win-win solutions instead of compromise. And the more that couples embody secure attachment before conflicts arise, the more optimally they tend to respond, making it a lot less likely that anyone's threat response is kicked off in the process.

Stable Connection. For all of these reasons (and many more), securely attached couples don't usually leave their relationships easily. They often stay together for a very long time; their commitment is durable and positive. Of course, divorces do happen, and death certainly separates people from one another, but it takes quite a bit to break up a securely attached couple. There's just so much benefit to remaining together.

I'm probably leaving a lot off this list, but you get the picture. For many people, this kind of relationship seems far-fetched or out of reach. However, most of us probably know at least one couple that exhibits the above qualities, at least in part. Let's try out Marion Solomon's idea about learning from mentor couples in the following exercise.

EXERCISE   **Mentor Couples**

Does the preceding list remind you of anyone you know? Take a moment to think about it. Who are the couples in your life—anyone you've known or observed—who seem to have these qualities? They don't need to perfectly fit this description all the time, but when you think about these couples, you're struck by their connection, playfulness, mutual protection, and general sense of well-being. Take a few minutes to think about who best represents these qualities to you. If asked, these securely attached couples may be willing to actively mentor you and your partner when troubles divide you. Or they may help you find more aliveness and joy to share to enhance what you already have. What a great source of useful tried-and-true advice!

Some of us might find it difficult to bring anyone to mind, and if that's true for you, go ahead and think about securely attached couples from fiction, TV, or movies. I mentioned the movie *Brooklyn* earlier. There's another one, called *Lion*, in which a young man searches for his birth mother while reassuring and acting in a loving way toward his adoptive mother. The two families open their hearts to one another, and it's a wonderful cinematic presentation of secure attachment. We all need some priming toward secure attachment, so see what examples you can come up with—it doesn't matter where they come from—and think about all the fabulous qualities in these relationships. Let yourself soak in that positivity. Absorb it as much as you can and open yourself to being changed by the natural power of secure attachment.

SECURE PARTNER PLUS INSECURE PARTNER

Although securely attached people may tend to bond together, it isn't uncommon for one to partner with a person with insecure attachment. For the latter, it's like hitting the jackpot, because the level of stability and healing that comes from being involved with a securely attached person is significant and precious. The insecure partner benefits by becoming reprogrammed by the consistent, healthy responsiveness of the securely attached person, and research shows that in as little as two to four years, they can become much more securely attached themselves.[7] It really doesn't matter what style is most dominant for you—avoidant, ambivalent, or disorganized—living in intimate relationship with a securely attached person is of obvious benefit. It is also a huge plus when two people get together who are both willing to work toward secure attachment by learning and practicing secure attachment skillfulness.

INSECURELY ATTACHED COUPLES

Of course, insecurely attached people are also attracted to each other, for several apparent and paradoxical reasons. Quite regularly, avoidant people and those with the ambivalent adaptation will pair up, or either of these styles will match up with someone who is disorganized. It can be tricky when avoidants and ambivalents get together, especially if there's a big variance in commitment to the relationship. When things get rocky, avoidants typically find relief and safety in isolation and distance, whereas ambivalents want more closeness. It takes a lot of education, compassionate awareness, and commitment to bridge these gaps because they tend to trigger each other toward their most painful wounds and increase insecurity versus diminish it.

Two avoidant people don't often stick together as a couple, simply because there's not enough glue to keep them together, so to speak. They're both so interested in parallel attention and being involved in their own inner life that it's difficult for either of them to build much of a bridge to the other person or to maintain that kind of connection over time. And disorganized couples have quite a challenging time staying together because they tend to trigger each other a lot. When both people are activated and distressed on a regular basis, they typically view the other person as an enemy, and it can feel something like a war zone. People understandably tend to leave situations that feel dangerous (with some exceptions, of course). However, even a couple with two disorganized partners can make it work if they aren't usually triggered at the same time, and one partner can remain more regulated. If one partner can play the role of being calm, safe, and stable, it can help the triggered partner move through their feelings of threat and terror to reconnect toward love and intimacy. This role may shift back and forth between partners.

●●

This gives you a cursory idea of what different matchups look like, although it's obviously much more complicated than I can summarize in a few paragraphs. What's more important is learning to work optimally with your partner of choice, but before I offer some practical suggestions, I don't want to jump the gun. Let's first assume that you don't have a partner and would like one. (If you're already in a relationship, feel free to skip ahead to "Making Your Relationship More Secure" on page 165.)

FINDING A PARTNER

Most of the ways we go about choosing our romantic relationships tend to involve physical attraction, common interests and values, or cultural factors such as socioeconomic status, family ties, and ethnicity. All around the world, women and men of various communities are taught from an early age who is most desirable as a partner, and that largely determines who they'll look for in a mate (or in some cases, who will be chosen for them). Unfortunately, these approaches don't always work out well, as most of us already know. To use some obvious examples: good looks, athletic prowess, and piles of money don't necessarily correlate with relational abilities.

We can also be unconsciously attracted to people who fit our relational template from childhood, and like puzzle pieces, we may connect with someone in a relationship who "fits" and who eventually triggers us to feel our unresolved issues with our parents. Many couples therapists see this situation as an opportunity for growth and healing for both partners.

People who are insecurely attached can sometimes find securely attached people boring: they don't present enough drama or *oomph*. For this reason, they often overlook securely attached people as potential partners, and that's a shame and a huge loss. I advise spending some time investigating those people who might not initially come across as exciting to see if they are consistently available, caring, affectionate, loyal, unflappable, present, responsive, and protective. These qualities are far more important in the long run than simply being crazy about someone at first sight. You can ask about their family background. Was it rich in connection, pro-social, and secure? This could be a big plus.

There's nothing wrong with being attracted to your potential partner, of course, but I suggest you learn to scan for secure attachment, or at least for insecure partners willing to move in that direction. The first year or so of a new relationship is basically one big chemical cocktail party happening in our body. We have all this bond-inducing oxytocin running through our system, and its function is to encourage connection, adoration, and attraction. Unfortunately, during this time, we are often blind to some crucial information about our partner and the way our relationship is unfolding. Stan Tatkin emphasizes the critical priority of vetting your partners with your friends or mentor couples because they often can see how you are together more clearly.[8] In addition, you can practice secure attachment skills to see how a new partner responds. This section is about entering whatever new relationship you choose with eyes open and new tools at the ready. As you become clearer about what really works for you in a relationship, you may choose to continue or leave with more clarity.

Seeking the Positive

At this point, my suggestion to look for signs of secure attachment won't come as any surprise. Securely attached people don't look a certain way, however, nor do they participate in particular activities, follow certain religions, or have specific cars or jobs. They just have a natural capacity to connect and reciprocate, and that's what I recommend looking for. But how?

I suggest a more organic approach to make the whole dating process less stressful and more efficient. So if you're interested in finding a securely attached person or a person willing to grow in that direction to spend your life with, I invite you to consider the following practices, many of which are adapted from the work of Amir Levine and Rachel Heller,[9] when meeting potential partners:

> **Don't play games.** Forget insincere strategizing. Standard dating advice recommends that you don't follow up too soon after your first encounter or that you hold off responding to the other person's first call or text until a day or two later. I guess the idea is that you don't want to come across as *too* interested, but that doesn't work with securely attached people. Believe it or not, they actually want to see early signs of connection; they're not interested in playing games. If someone is put off by you being responsive and attentive early on, chances are they're not securely attached.

> **Express your needs early.** Some people are nervous about talking about their needs too early in a relationship;

they're afraid it might be a turnoff. If we're insecurely attached, we can feel like our needs will be perceived by others as a burden, so we're a little wary about how we express ourself. I recommend doing something different because you need to look for consistent responsiveness early on, and that's just not information you can get from others unless you give them the opportunity.[10] So try it out and see how your potential partner handles being with someone (*you*) who actually has their own needs. Likewise, are you responsive to the other's needs? For all of these qualities, you can observe your own inclinations as well.

Assess responsiveness. You can find out quite a bit by taking note of how long it takes a person to respond to texts, emails, and calls. I'm not talking about keeping score, and it isn't realistic to expect people to respond immediately all the time—we all have work and other demands to attend to. But you can detect patterns in responsiveness fairly early on, and that will tell you a lot about what the person will be like in the long run. If they have to break a date, do they apologize, explain, and reschedule? Or do they leave you hanging?

Watch how they treat you. What happens when you go out together? Does your new partner treat you like the special person you are in public, or do they ignore you or criticize you for one thing or another? Watch for signs of protection, as well. You're looking for evidence that they're interested in keeping you safe in the world, protecting you from harm, and that they're not going to abandon you or turn on you should things go a little sideways. Do they avoid hurtful actions and unkind words? How generous are they? How often do they initiate repair attempts when misunderstandings occur? How much do they notice and appreciate your efforts and displays of affection?

Take a trip together. If you're able to do so, I recommend going away for a few days together when the time feels right. It's a great way to learn some important things about your partner, as well as the relationship itself. Do they help make the arrangements, share the costs and responsibilities, help carry the luggage, or participate equally in other ways? Are they interested in sharing some of the same activities as you are, or do they only invite you along to join them in activities they want to do? Check out the balance of your time alone and your time together. Are the transitions between those points smooth, or do they feel contentious and tense? Does one of you need to be by yourself a lot more than the other person? None of this should be viewed as finalizing evidence, by the way; it's just important information that will help you determine if you want to move forward in the relationship.

Consider the conflicts. Disagreements, misattunements, and conflicts happen in any relationship. It's actually helpful to have these things come up early on because they tell you a lot about what kind of partnership you might have with the person. Do they express themselves in a way that makes sense to you? Do they apologize or take responsibility for what might be their contribution to the difficulty? Are they interested in understanding your side of things, or are they mostly invested in being right? How open are they in repairing whatever little rifts come up? Do they readily accept your apology when needed? You can also look for their willingness to be flexible and perhaps shift behaviors that will support the relationship better. What are they like when conflicts get a little heated and difficult—argumentative and hurtful, or patient and considerate? I hope it goes without saying that you should be examining your own behavior in this way, too.

View the verbals (and nonverbals). Consider the language your partner uses to convey their feelings and points of view. Also pay attention to their tone of voice. Is it soothing and melodic, or monotone and harsh? Do they look at you with kindness and appreciation? Is their face mobile and expressive? In what ways do they convey affection and safety with their touch? Take what you've learned throughout this book and pay close attention to your partner's language, tone, eye contact, expressions, and gestures with great interest.

Red Flags

There are specific things to watch out for that will be evident from the previous list of practices. I also want to note some things that are tip-offs as to whether someone leans avoidant, ambivalent, or disorganized. The following lists for avoidant and ambivalent are partially adapted from the work of Amir Levine and Rachel Heller.[11] These lists aren't comprehensive, and none of the points should be used to disqualify your love interest outright. Please don't make any snap decisions based on one or two experiences; just look for clues and patterns along the way. All of this is merely information to take into account when you examine the big picture and are making a decision about your level of investment in a future together. It takes time to observe others well. A difficult response (or one you find unacceptable) may be an anomaly; it could also indicate a well-worn pattern. The most important thing is to find a potential partner who is open and willing to work toward secure attachment (whether they know that terminology or not). Finding a person with that committed inclination is pure gold.

Possible Markers for People with the Avoidant Adaptation

- Your partner is put off when you express your needs. In other words, they treat your needs as a problem.

- They feel they can best meet their own needs by themselves.

- You often feel that you have to pull words out of their mouth. At worst, they seem secretive and withholding.

- They habitually engage in distancing behaviors. They need a lot of space, and this need seems to increase as the relationship progresses and you get closer.

- They regularly drop off the radar. They don't respond to your texts or calls in any consistent way.

- Intimacy does not beget more intimacy, but instead they close off or withdraw after closeness.

- They're regularly negative, critical, or dismissive. You detect a lot of fault-finding behavior, especially directed your way.

- They idealize ex-partners or future partners. After gaining some distance from former relationships, they can access the love and connection they had because the pressure is off their attachment system. Likewise, when imagining the perfect future mate, they are not currently dealing with their need for distance to feel safe. In these scenarios, they are not in the trenches of an actual relationship.

- They seem to have unrealistic notions of romance. They're surprised and taken aback by normal ups and downs and often don't handle conflicts in a helpful way.

- They aren't willing to express their affection or openly commit. They may withhold touch and verbal affirmation. They don't easily say "I love you" or other things that express their appreciation and care for you.

Possible Markers for People with the Ambivalent Adaptation

- They seem habitually insecure or clingy. Lacking object constancy, they regularly need reassurance in one form or another that you are there for them.

- They have a tendency toward jealousy. They're regularly looking for evidence of abandonment and may suspect you of infidelity when it is not true.

- Even after some time, your partner has a difficult time trusting you. They may listen in on your conversations, go through your texts, or read your emails looking for proof that you're more interested in someone else.

- They're hyperfocused on you and underfocused on themselves. They may not practice good self-care and may try to take care of you in a way that ties you to them.

- They play games, keep score, act in manipulative ways, and seem to pick fights. At times, it seems they are unintentionally pushing you away out of fear of looming rejection, even when you are clearly committed.

- They can be intensely emotional on a regular basis—becoming sad, disappointed, or angry at you even preceding any obvious rift between you.

- They may express ambivalence by wanting you close and then pushing you away.

- They chronically complain and ignore your caring behaviors due to the need to keep the signal cry on. They may talk excessively to feel connected.

- They have trouble letting go of old wounds or conflicts in the relationship to focus on the needed solutions now.

Possible Markers for People with the Disorganized Adaptation

- Look for extreme swings between the behaviors listed for the avoidant and ambivalent adaptations, mixed with fear. For example, they sometimes keep their distance from you but need a lot of reassurance and attention at other times, and they struggle with defensiveness and dysregulation.

- They experience the freeze response, seem dissociated, and may have gaps in their memory. They may start sentences and not finish them or speak in a way that is hard to follow — mixing tenses or losing words.

- They display strong triggers that seem to come out of nowhere. It can be hard to make sense of what makes them upset.

- When triggered, they may become confused and unable to make even simple decisions. Fewer choices, described with clarity, can be helpful.

- At a certain point in the relationship, they may begin to experience inexplicable terror, especially when related to increasing intimacy and safety with you.

If you're looking for a long-term partner, I hope these guidelines will help. If you can see what's coming, it will empower you to make better decisions for yourself and hopefully help you steer clear of too many obvious challenges. As well, it's ideal that you exhibit secure attachment skills yourself and communicate your growing capacity to partners the best you can. Remember how important it is for both partners to be compassionately aware of their own strengths and limitations (as well as those of their partner) and remain willing to work toward learning secure attachment skills. Once you're in a committed relationship, the following section will help you boost your satisfaction and deepen the relationship further.

MAKING YOUR RELATIONSHIP MORE SECURE

When you've established an attachment bond with another person, it means that you have essentially become their primary attachment figure, and they have become yours. This is true even when you're in conflict, are unhappy with one another, or are in different parts of the world. On a fundamental level, we're oriented toward a primary attachment figure. We are built for connection for our entire life; it's not something that goes away. Accordingly, it's a good idea to keep that bond with our significant other in good condition and make it stronger over time. Certainly we can eventually detach from a negative influence; we may leave a relationship and find a new partner who becomes our new primary attachment figure. We may shift our attachment adaptation more and more toward secure in our relationships with others in general, especially when we learn secure attachment skills. We can all understand our partners and ourselves more compassionately and learn how to be together more securely.

Stan Tatkin and Tracey Boldemann-Tatkin's work, which I mentioned in the introduction, is so important in this way, and I highly recommend their books and audio programs for the public, their couple's weekends, and their specialized PACT trainings for therapists. Because our primary bonds are so meaningful, it's crucial that we know our partners well, be able to bring them up when they're down, calm them when they're stressed, and do our best to help them through all the nuances of being alive. Of course, we want them to pay attention to us and care for us in this way, too, because both partners have a sacred responsibility to promote each other's well-being. Ideally, both people are working to co-regulate one another while helping the other person with whatever it takes to self-soothe.

By now, I hope you have a good idea of what secure attachment looks like and how to practice secure attachment skills (the SAS I spelled out in chapter one) for yourself and others. I won't review that material here, but I recommend trying out these skills with everyone important in your life. For now, it might also be helpful to look at how to work, and grow, with partners who express one or more forms of insecure attachment.

Growing with Avoidant Partners

You'll recall that people with the avoidant style grew up with some level of neglect or active rejection. Either their parents were consistently non-responsive, lacked presence in a substantial way, or simply weren't attuned to their child's needs—specifically their emotional needs. When this child becomes an adult, their attachment system is active, but they unconsciously put the brakes on. This is a natural response when you grow up with neglect, because your survival requires it. It's simply too painful to stay open to connect when no one is there for you or they repsond negatively to your needs or presence.

That being said, attachment is also a biological need. It's an instinct because we're actually safer when we're connected to others. We're more regulated, more satisfied, and more resourced. So it takes a lot of energy to impede the attachment system from doing what it naturally wants to do, and those of us who are avoidant usually don't notice that we're working so hard to stop our inclination to connect when we're used to putting the brakes on.

An avoidant person who enters into a connective relationship is taking an incredible risk. They might seem to have it all together, but beneath that calm exterior, they're dealing with all these warning bells telling them that getting closer to others will result in rejection or hurt or loss. Try to keep this in mind and recognize their incredible sensitivity and vulnerability. As a child, they were shunned, neglected, or rejected in some way—so much so that they had to disconnect from their relational environment in order to take care of themselves. Basically, there was not enough of a positive holding environment to connect to in those formative times. Their young nervous system did not have the opportunity to learn to interactively regulate with a calm, present adult, so they missed the calming, pleasurable effects of co-regulation. So when they choose to reach out and connect to others, it's a really big deal for them.

For avoidants, relational growth requires dealing with a lot of emotional pain, which means they have to let go and work through a lot of numbing or deactivating attachment strategies they picked up along the way. It can sometimes prove challenging to work with avoidants because they are not always oriented toward seeking help or even understanding their internal experience very well. Keep in mind that their nervous system did not have an adequate opportunity for interactive regulation as a child, and learning to access that type or regulation is significant for their healing.

Avoidant people really need the benefit of the doubt. To move toward secure attachment, they need your support and recognition; they need you to meet their thoughts, feelings, and physical body with love and tenderness. It might be hard to see it sometimes, but avoidants have a lot happening on the inside, and they need more time than others to shift back into contact with you. Additionally, they may not be attentive to social cues (or may regularly misinterpret them), and they may not signal so well themselves.

It is important to respect and support their need for transition because they aren't adept at moving from aloneness to connection. As I mentioned in chapter two, it's a stressful shift for them, which explains why they can sometimes come across as dismissive, agitated, or angry. When this occurs, try to remember all that's going on for them and do your best to not take their bristliness personally. That's what I mean when I say give them the benefit of the doubt. They are capable of loving, but sometimes they need to turn off their attachment system to feel safe. This tendency diminishes when they access more of the nourishment available through secure attachment.

If you give avoidants their space and respect the time it takes them to shift back into relationship with you, it will feel a lot less like trying to hug a porcupine. I'm not saying that you shouldn't have any personal reactions to their process, just that you try to be as available, understanding, and nourishing as possible. When avoidant people begin to feel safe on an emotional and physiological level, they come to realize that relationships are worthwhile, and they begin to value connection in ways they never thought possible. To this end, it can also be useful to help them identify their needs, or at least anticipate their needs yourself, because avoidants are not usually skilled at knowing what they need in the moment or allowing and seeking others to help them.

Growing with Ambivalent Partners

In contrast, people with ambivalent attachment may have been often taken care of and loved as children, but their caregivers did so in a notably unpredictable and inconsistent way. As kids, they were never sure which parent was going to show up—the loving and attentive parent or the absent and distracted one (including parents who were overly preoccupied and distracted by their own attachment wounds). This on again/off again parenting style disturbs a stable, relaxed connection, increasing anxiety and sensitivity to any perceived or projected slight. Whereas the avoidant person was left alone too much with too little nourishing interaction with a caring parental presence, the ambivalent person may have been loved, then habitually overstimulated and/ or intermittently abandoned. Ambivalents experienced intrusion or interrupted affect modulation on a regular basis, meaning they did not have the benefit of parents or caretakers who could help them contain or express emotions in a regulated way. So as adults they have difficulty feeling a wide range of emotions in a way that is modulated and manageable. For these reasons, ambivalent people strongly yearn for stable connection but are not always adept at recognizing when a relationship is supportive, loving, and worthy of their deepening trust. They may miss caring behaviors from partners or may actively reject what they say they want, pushing away the people they most want to be close to in their lives. They need to learn how to receive love and attention and to experience fulfillment and satisfaction without the disabling fear of losing the relationship.

If you offer an ambivalent person reassurance on a regular basis, it will go a long way to calming down their attachment system. When they're activated and scared about losing you, they can act in ways that might jeopardize the relationship simply because they're experiencing such intense fear. I highly advise not tripping that wire because it can be quite difficult for an ambivalent person to come back from the depths of their fear of abandonment. Do your best to not respond reactively to their attachment paradox and help them calm down. Do not threaten to leave or to end the relationship. Once they know that things are safe and that you're really going to be there for them, their attachment system won't scream as loudly or as regularly for connection.

If you're not going to be as available as usual in your relationship with an ambivalent person—maybe you have to travel out of town or you're simply occupied temporarily with work—make a point of staying tethered to them in some way. Make the best use of all of this technology we have available to us—call, text, email, Skype, FaceTime—do whatever helps you both feel connected even when you can't be together as you normally might. If you remind your ambivalent partner that you're there for them, that you love and miss them, that you value them deeply, that they're incredibly important to you, that they're the person you most want to spend your life with, that you can't wait to see them again—well, you'll be surprised at how far supportive reassurance goes.

And if you can balance your life in such a way that your ambivalent partner knows that you are available to them, it will go a long way to calm down any jealous behaviors on their part. It doesn't matter whether they're suspicious of your friends, work, or hobbies; what matters is that you let them know in tangible ways how important they are to you. If you do this, they won't feel so distressed if you are occasionally not available. When you water the seeds of secure attachment, your partner can relax, and they won't need as much reassurance as they once did. They need to know they are important to you—ideally your top priority.

When ambivalent people calm down, become more relaxed, and find a way to trust the connection between you, they'll move toward secure attachment, and both of you will reap the benefits of that. As their insecurities dissolve, they'll be able to access more self-soothing, they'll move toward you and deepen their commitment, and they'll want to treat you like royalty—the best of the best.

Growing with Disorganized Partners

A partner with disorganized attachment does want to connect with you and feel safe, but their threat response became wired in to their need for attachment at an early age. Remember that they come by this situation tragically and honestly: in one way or another, they're a survivor of a threatening attachment experience before they could even make sense of it. In addition, it's probable that up to this point in their life, they haven't spent much time with anyone who has been able to help them regulate their nervous system. People with disorganized adaptation feel their feelings much more intensely because of this; they simply haven't developed the neurological resources to handle them.

Your primary goal is to meet their fear with messages of safety and regulation. Even something as simple as a whole-bodied belly-to-belly hug is extremely regulating. No matter how you do it, be there in the best way you can that helps them calm down from anxious states and to up-regulate from depressive, shut-down places. To this end, it's important to create safe havens, even safe rituals, to employ when your partner becomes distressed. Maybe they don't say anything, but they give you a certain gesture or look that lets you know they want you to come and hold them. Or perhaps you rest your foot on top of theirs to help them feel more grounded when they're triggered into dysregulation. Or if you have a clue that some activation is about to kick off, you find a straightforward way to connect and co-regulate before the storm comes. You can also try using a transitional object—something special such as a precious piece of jewelry or a favorite figurine—that you give your partner when you're going to be gone for a while or when your partner is feeling particularly distressed. If you're with your partner for a long time, you'll naturally collect cues as to what works for them and what doesn't. In a very real way, you're putting together a handbook on your partner—a field guide, of sorts.

Mostly it's important to let your partner know that you're a safe person to be close to. If they project any type of threat onto you—as they might from time to time—it's important that it doesn't last long. Safe touch is a wonderful tool, and words can also go a long way when this type of thing comes up. Try saying, "You're safe with me. I care about you. I want to help you with your feelings, and I'm here when you're ready. If you need space, that's okay too, just let me know when you need me." Do your best to help them come out of whatever extreme state they're in. If you're there on a consistent basis and help them reduce their suffering, it will gradually bring them more into secure attachment, and you'll be able to enjoy a quality relationship much more easily. It might take some time to make this happen, but it's especially beautiful to witness someone with disorganized attachment learn to self-regulate and heal. Of course it is important that they support you in these ways, too.

WORKING WITH YOUR OWN ATTACHMENT STYLE

I want to reiterate that your attachment style—and that of everyone else—comes from early patterning that is almost entirely unconscious and imprinted in the body. We don't often recognize our adaptations until adulthood when particular patterns show up across relationships, or maybe we've been able to learn about this part of ourself through therapy, in meditation retreats, from self-reflection, through feedback from partners, or in other ways. If we had childhood traumas, those can also get kicked up seemingly out of nowhere. Sometimes these occurrences have a direct link to our attachment injuries, and sometimes they're triggered by additional traumas that happen to us as adults—accidents, assaults, sudden losses, and so on.

Regardless of how we experience these episodes and patterns—and especially when it comes to insecure attachment—it's important to remember that they aren't our fault. For whatever reason, life dished out something less than ideal, and it got embedded in us physiologically. Our attachment style isn't something that we can talk or wish our way out of; it's deep inside of us, and it is always active automatically. For this reason, it is crucial to have compassion for yourself. We need to have compassion for others too, of course, but it's critical that compassion begins at home.

When you're in a relationship with someone, be sure to practice self-care whenever you feel something difficult arising. One simple way to do this is to take a time-out when you need one. Things get heated from time to time, and it can serve you to let things cool down a little before resolving a conflict. Take a break from your partner, go for a walk in the forest, call a friend for support, call your therapist, get a little more grounded, and then contact your partner to see if they're willing and ready to repair. Let them know how long you will be gone and when they can expect your return.

Here's an additional (and maybe unusual) self-care practice you can do when you feel tension or discomfort starting to arise.

EXERCISE   Investigating Discomfort

Whatever your brand of discomfort is—maybe you feel inexplicably stressed when your partner approaches you physically, or you get anxious when your partner is about to leave for a few days—feel the pain, lean into it, and stay with it for as long as you can in a manageable way. This might be exactly the opposite of what you find yourself wanting to do, and that's okay! Just try it out. I think you'll be surprised by what happens.

To be clear, I'm not talking about diving into sensations of being overwhelmed and masochistically sticking with that experience no matter what. Instead, I'm referring here to the initial waves of discomfort—that growing pit in your stomach, the slight headache above your ears, the tension in your chest or shoulders, or that indeterminate, unlocatable sense of dread as it begins to come on. The next time something like this happens, try this exercise before you engage in your usual self-care strategies.

Locate the discomfort in your body. Where is it exactly? Does it stay in one place, move around, come and go? Get curious about its shape and texture. Be open to looking at your discomfort in a tangible way that might be entirely new to you.

Notice that the sensations are occurring entirely in your body. Consider that all of what you are feeling arises from within. Try on the thought that your discomfort isn't about your partner, but about your attachment history. That's the source of your discomfort. If you notice any resistance to this step, that's okay too. Just notice whatever sensations arise from that resistance. Are they different than your initial discomfort? What are they like?

Feel what's happening now in your body. Recognize these feelings as your attachment history showing up the only way it knows how. Say hello to it. Give it a seat at the table. Open your heart to it and hear what it has to say. What does it want to tell you?

Check in with your body again. Has anything changed? Have the sensations become stronger or weaker? Have they moved somewhere else in your body? Do you note any different sensations, perhaps any associated with relaxation and well-being?

Whatever happens during this practice, welcome it as best you can with kind attention. If things get too intense, it's okay to stop. You can switch your focus to a personal activity that is deeply stabilizing—a resource tht brings you relief and regulation. It can be a powerful act of compassion to take a break and try again at some other time.

Regardless of your attachment history, life isn't always a struggle. We all experience splashes and waves of goodness, happiness, and contentment, albeit sometimes way more fleeting than we'd like. And even those of us in difficult relationships can feel connected with our partner, grounded, and calm from time to time. Those moments are important to note. Our brain and nervous systems focus on negative experiences quite a bit: otherwise, we'd never have been vigilant enough to have made it as a species. As I've mentioned, Rick Hanson (and many others) notes that reprogramming old wounds requires recognizing what's going well in your life—safety, protection, happiness, and so on.[12] Life is made of this stuff, too, and recognizing that fact will enable us to relieve habitual distress and connect to others in healthy, boundaried ways. In order to repattern our tendency to focus on the negative, it's important to note the positive as it arises, really pay attention to the experience for longer than we're accustomed to, and let our neuroplasticity do its work. I recommend at least 15 to 30 seconds, or longer, if possible. We can actually alter our brain in this way and tune in to our natural frequency of secure attachment.

Finally, for some of us there can certainly be a "fake it till you make it" aspect to our secure attachment journey. We all act in ways we don't like sometimes, and it especially hurts when we do so with people who are dear to us. Do your best to accept the fact that such times are unavoidable, but also know that you're not stuck in some narrow behavioral script determined by your caregivers a long time ago. It's also good medicine to practice the secure attachment skills (SAS) whenever you can, especially in your relationships. And, as

I mentioned before, if you're someone who's looking for a securely attached partner, trying out these skills yourself will increase your chances of attracting one and establishing a nourishing relationship. To this end, review chapter one and the list at the beginning of this chapter that describes what securely attached couples look like. Don't think that you have to try everything on at once; just find a couple of attributes and techniques that come most naturally to you and resonate with the gifts you already bring into relationship.

SAYING GOODBYE TO A RELATIONSHIP

Unfortunately, it's not always possible to stay in partnership. Sometimes it's not the best decision to continue to work to keep the relationship intact. And sometimes we have to make the decision to move on, learn from the experience, heal as much as possible, and try again. Before I list the following considerations (also partially from the work of Amir Levine and Rachel Heller[13]), I want to be absolutely clear that these types of decisions can only be made by you. Neither I nor any other professional should ever suggest that you make choices that contradict your own intelligence and sense of integrity. The following difficulties might ring true in your experience of your current relationship, but that's not to say that I recommend moving on. As with all choices in life, this one is yours to make. I offer this list merely as points to consider from an attachment perspective and with the recognition that relationships are far more complex than any particular lens can describe or elucidate.

With that being said, here are some things to consider that might indicate that your relationship is less than ideal:

- You regularly feel some distress about your relationship.

- You're constantly fighting, or the fights you have are habitual and never seem to get anywhere.

- Periods of closeness are typically followed by drastic shifts into conflict and distance. It never seems like you can settle in to a state of satisfaction, healing, and nourishment.

- You have strong, ongoing doubts about you and your partner's capacity for closeness. There's too much ongoing variance between the two of you in the desire for connection and the need for distance.

- Your partner isn't available for positive change. Either they're shut off or overly invested in their own anxiety and struggles.

- There is a significant imbalance between you when it comes to communication, participation in the relationship, and generosity—that is, being willing to freely give to each other and the relationship itself.

- You feel like you have become the enemy and not the beloved to your partner. Your partner seems happier with and confides more in their friends and family.

- One of you wants an exclusive, monogamous relationship and the other wants an open polyamorous relationship and you cannot reach a workable outcome.

Ideally, you have found someone who is committed to mutual growth, evolution, and healthy relationship. Not everyone has that interest or capacity, unfortunately, and it's up to you to make an evaluation of whether there's enough to work with. Relationships can be difficult under even the best of circumstances, so it's important that both people have shared buy-in. However, before you make any final decisions, I think it's always a good idea to do what you can to improve your own secure capacities. That can take a while, of course, but it will go a long way to helping you assess the relationship. And if it ends up not working out for your current relationship, you will have routed yourself in a positive direction toward gaining a securely attached partnership in the future.

A FINAL WORD

No matter where you find yourself on this journey, I hope you find a way to increase enjoyment in your life, to find presence and playfulness and protection in the company of others, and to deeply feel all the love and connection that is your birthright. Whether couples are in same-sex relationships or heterosexual, my enduring wish is that we all learn to love freely, to love better, and to receive the same from others. For me, that's what working with these attachment adaptations is all about.

As we move toward secure attachment, our natural capacities come to the forefront. We're more compassionate toward ourself and others; we develop a healthy sense of self, while at the same time becoming more selfless. We expand our capacity for brain integration, and all the benefits of the various parts of ourself come together. We can attune to ourself, but also to others. Our prefrontal cortex matures and becomes more developed, and that sensitivity to ourselves and others is good for all of us. Over time, there isn't such a division between taking care of ourself, attending to others, nourishing our community, and nurturing our planet. We become global and ecofriendly citizens interested in what's good for all of us. We no longer view the world solely through the lens of scarcity and competition, but we collaborate with spacious understanding and expansive care toward all life.

Imagine the possibilities. Think about how different the world would be if every leader had some understanding of secure attachment, how to treat others with respect and dignity, how to resolve conflicts for mutual benefit, how to negotiate different needs and interests, and how to live with wonder, appreciation, and love. I know, it's a tall order, but I believe the dream is possible. With understanding secure attachment and learning its markers and skills, all of this is possible, and more.

It's all right here within us. We're hardwired for secure attachment; we have the equipment. Deep down, all of us are designed for intimacy, connection, awareness, and love. We're amazing, magical creatures, and to see each other as such is a tremendous gift to everyone involved. Open yourself to that. Open yourself to all that it means to become fully human, fully who you were meant to be. You can do it. We all can do it. We're designed to do it.

ACKNOWLEDGMENTS

I could fill this entire book with the names and accomplishments of people to whom I owe gratitude and appreciation. The following list is in no way comprehensive, and I apologize in advance to anyone I've left out. I thank all of you frequently in my heart, even if I fail to do so in print now.

First of all, I want to thank the genius shining through Peter Levine in his lifelong search to alleviate human suffering, culminating in Somatic Experiencing (SE). Peter was instrumental in my own personal healing journey from extreme trauma toward regaining resiliency and enhancing a deep understanding that supported my professional endeavors and insights all along the way. I want to thank his past and present SE faculty—especially those friends I worked most closely with: Nancy Napier, Maggie Phillips, Raja Selvam, Marianne Bentzen, Anngwyn St. Just, Steve Hoskinson, Larry Heller, and Kathy Kain. I also want to send my appreciation to the amazing Somatic Experiencing staff at SETI and Ergos Institute, specifically Justin Snavely.

I also owe a huge debt to the greats of attachment theory, as well as the amazing therapists, authors, and researchers doing incredible work in the fields of trauma recovery and enhancing connection and healing in relationships—John Bowlby, Mary Ainsworth, Mary Main, Marion Solomon, Ed Tronick, Allan Schore, Sue Johnson, Maggie Phillips, Diana Fosha, David Wallin, Amir Levine, Rachel Heller, Stan Tatkin, Tracey Boldemann-Tatkin, Ellyn Bader, Peter Pearson, Terry Real, Pat Love, Michele Wiener-Davis, Joan Borysenko, Linda Graham, Lisa Ferenz, Mary Jo Barrett, Bill O'Hanlon, Peter Cummings, David Grand, Bruce Ecker, Frank Anderson, Richard Schwartz, John Howard, Rachel Cahn, and Jeff Pincus. I am blessed that so many are current collaborators. I offer my eternal admiration and gratitude to all of you.

I also want to thank Stephen Porges for his intelligence, warmth, and revolutionary research that underlies so much somatic work being done today. On that note, I extend my gratitude to the brilliance of Dan Siegel, Bonnie Badenoch, Janina Fisher, Pat Ogden, Rick Hanson, Bessel van der Kolk, Robert Scaer, Babette Rothschild, Belleruth Naparstek, Ray Castellino, Bonnie Mark-Goldstein, and John and Anna Chitty for their furtherance of effectively using somatic strategies as well as neuroscience for trauma resolution and the understanding of the critical importance of healing attachment injury. I also give thanks to John Bilorusky for providing me with excellent guidance during my PhD studies at Western Institute for Social Research (WISR).

I want to heartfully offer my gratitude to my co-teachers of the Dynamic Attachment Re-patterning experience (DARe) and Somatic Attachment Training experience (SATe) professional training programs: Patti Elledge, Patricia Meadows, Elisabeth Schneider-Kaiser, Alicen Halquist, Sara Swift, and Judith Beermann Zeligson as well as countless dedicated assistants including but in no way limited to Jennifer Jonell, Wanda Brothers, Margaret Crockett, Jane Cohen, Wendy Hubbard, Teri Sullivan Lutz, Gil Shalit, Daniel Vose, Martha Brandt, Kirtan Coan, Erin Brandt, Cathy Latner, Char Dillon, Linda Chrisman, Amar Huang, Patricia McKay, Lars Johansen, Sabina Scheffler, Heidi Wittkop, Najakat Ute Kalinke, Marianne Mueller, and Ellen Stautenberg. And I am forever grateful for and indebted to my Trauma Solutions staff, who always have my back. Each one offers me ongoing support in too many ways to elucidate here: Mary Niebch, Tim Coyle, Jennifer Jonell, and Kristine Parrinello. I also would like to thank Eben Pagan, Jeff Walker, and Ruth Buczynski for helping me learn to deliver educational value with integrity, and my many colleagues and associates who make my work possible: Brian Spielmann (including his partner, Richard Taubinger) and able staff—Ian MacPherson, Asa Henderson, Artem Nikulkov, as well as Felix, Erik, and Katy. Thanks so much to Jacqueline Carleton and her team of interns, Myriam Schottenstein and Diana Scime-Sayegh, for their help in organizing transcripts and materials from live trainings for professional writings to come. I also extend my lasting gratitude to the good people at Sounds True: Tami Simon, who invited me to publish two books; Stephen Lessard and his team for their work on the audio program *Healing Your Attachment Wounds*; and Robert Lee for his expertise in writing, organizing, and editing that material to create the book you're reading now.

I want to recognize and celebrate all of the teachers, guides, allies, and co-explorers who have been with me along my spiritual journey: Laurel Keyes, Paul Chivington, Kurt Leland, Hameed Ali, Faisal Muqaddam, Morton and Deborah Letofsky, Linda Krier, Prabha Bell, Amano Atwood, Carolyn Tricomi, Nancy Napier, Neila Frisch, Rennie Moran, Gil Shalit, Manohar Croke, Christian Koln, Rani Willams, Velusia van Horsen, Darshana Mathews, Florian Usener, Najma Neuhoff, Madhurima Margit Rigtrup, Dominie Cappadonna, Sara Swift, William Allen, Anna Chitty, and the Dalai Lama. Thank you all!

My mother and father instilled in me an invaluable moral code that includes the value of education, the importance in helping others, and approaching life's challenges with an openhearted steadfastness. The consistency of their support as well as some of the inevitable struggles gave me the push I needed to explore my inner and outer world. I offer them my everlasting thanks. I also want to recognize the other members of my family who have been there for me in so many ways and who are inextricably woven into this journey: my siblings, Dick and Barb; my nieces, Andrea, Kelly, and Jessica; my nephew, Jason; my great nieces, Michaela and Mari; all of the spouses in the family, Barb, Jay, Zach, and Mike; my stepson, Kevin, and his family. I love you all so much.

Finally, I want to thank my many clients and students for giving me the great privilege of accompanying them on their amazing journeys of transforming trauma and mending broken connections. You have been my greatest teachers, and none of my work would be possible without you. I have been inspired and enriched by every encounter. Thank you all.

NOTES

Introduction

1. Stan Tatkin, *We Do: Saying Yes to a Relationship of Depth, True Connection, and Enduring Love* (Boulder, CO: Sounds True, 2018).

2. David McNamee, "Coma Patients Show Improved Recovery from Hearing Family Voices," Medical News Today, January 23, 2015, medicalnewstoday.com/articles/288463.php.

3. Simone Schnall et al., "Social Support and the Perception of Geographical Slant," *Journal of Experimental Social Psychology* 44, no. 5 (September 2008): 1246–1255, doi.org/10.1016/j.jesp.2008.04.011.

4. Marion Solomon and Stan Tatkin, *Love and War in Intimate Relationships: Connection, Disconnection, and Mutual Regulation in Couple Therapy* (New York: Norton, 2010).

5. Daniel J. Siegel, "Imagining Tomorrow: Healing and Hope in the Human Age" (keynote address with Diane Ackerman), March 28, 2015, Psychotherapy Networker Conference, Washington, DC.

6. *Oprah's SuperSoul Sessions*, episode 101, "Oprah Winfrey, Brené Brown & Tim Storey," aired December 13, 2015, on OWN network, oprah.com/own-supersoulsessions/oprah-winfrey-brene-brown--tim-storey.

7. Barbara Fredrickson, *Love 2.0: Finding Happiness and Health in Moments of Connection* (New York: Hudson Street Press, 2013).

8. Stephen Porges, "A moderated discussion of Stephen Porges' work, including a discussion of the clinical application of Polyvagal Theory," *Psychotherapy 2.0: Leading-Edge Discoveries on Neuroscience, Trauma, Mindfulness, and Attachment Therapy* (Sounds True webinar series), September 18, 2015.

9. Rick Hanson and Richard Mendius, *Buddha's Brain: The Practical Neuroscience of Happiness, Love, and Wisdom* (Oakland, CA: New Harbinger, 2009), 40–42.

10. Bruce Ecker, "Working with Implicit and Explicit Memory to Heal Trauma and Attachment," Therapy Mastermind Circle (webinar series with Diane Poole Heller), originally released August 8, 2017, dianepooleheller.com/working-implicit-explicit-memory-heal-trauma-attachment/.

11. Dan Siegel, "Dan Siegel: Me + We = Mwe," video, 1:29, February 8, 2016, youtube.com/watch?v=uo8Yo4UE6g0.

Chapter One: Secure Attachment

1. Edward Z. Tronick and Andrew Gianino, "Interactive Mismatch and Repair: Challenges to the Coping Infant," *Zero to Three* 6, no. 3 (February 1986): 1–6.

2. D. W. Winnicott, *Playing and Reality* (Abingdon, UK: Routledge, 1971).

3. Tronick and Gianino, "Interactive Mismatch and Repair," 1–6.

4. Daniel Goleman, "Three Kinds of Empathy: Cognitive, Emotional, Compassionate" (blog post), June 12, 2007, danielgoleman.info/three-kinds-of-empathy-cognitive-emotional-compassionate/.

5. Stan Tatkin, "Welcome Home Exercise for Couples," video, 4:05, September 23, 2009, youtube.com/watch?v=V9FBdC2Kykg; Marion Solomon and Stan Tatkin, *Love and War in Intimate Relationships: Connection, Disconnection, and Mutual Regulation in Couple Therapy* (New York: Norton, 2011).

6. Liz Burke, "This Is Why You Want to Rip Your Partner's Head Off," *New York Post*, July 2, 2017, nypost.com/2017/07/02/this-is-why-you-want-to-rip-your-partners-head-off/.

7. Sybil Carrere and John M. Gottman, "Predicting Divorce Among Newlyweds from the First Three Minutes of a Marital Conflict Discussion," *Family Process* 38, no. 3 (1999): 293–301, doi.org/10.1111/j.1545-5300.1999.00293.x.

8. Marjorie Beeghly and Ed Tronick, "Early Resilience in the Context of Parent-Infant Relationships: A Social Developmental Perspective," *Current Problems in Pediatric and Adolescent Health Care* 41, no 7 (August 2011): 197–201, doi.org/10.1016/j.cppeds.2011.02.005; Diane Poole Heller, "Practicing Relationship Repairs" (blog post), Sep 30, 2016, dianepooleheller.com/practicing-relationship-repairs/.

9. Caroline Myss, *Why People Don't Heal and How They Can* (New York: Three Rivers Press, 1997), 6.

10. Amir Levine, "Deciphering Attachment Styles in Everyday Life for Dating and Relationships" (keynote address), April 9, 2016, DARe to Connect: Attachment, Trauma & Intimacy Conference, Boulder, CO.

Chapter Two: Avoidant Attachment

1. Saul McCloud, "Mary Ainsworth," Simply Psychology, updated August 5, 2018, simplypsychology.org/mary-ainsworth.html.

2. "Disorganized Attachment: How Disorganized Attachments Form & How They Can Be Healed," Psych Alive, accessed September 1, 2018, psychalive.org/disorganized-attachment; Kendra Cherry, "The Story of Bowlby, Ainsworth, and Attachment Theory: The Importance of Early Emotional Bonds," Verywell Mind, February 19, 2018, verywellmind.com/what-is-attachment-theory-2795337.

3. Marion Solomon, *Lean on Me: The Power of Positive Dependency* (New York: Simon & Schuster, 1994).

Chapter Three: Ambivalent Attachment

1. Amir Levine and Rachel Heller, *Attached: The New Science of Adult Attachment and How It Can Help You Find—and Keep—Love* (New York: TarcherPerigee, 2012), 177–182.

2. ABC News, "Tips for Moms with Newborn Babies," *World News Now*, May 12, 2011, youtube.com/watch?v=G1g6ecQiw5I.

3. Stan Tatkin, *Wired for Love: How Understanding Your Partner's Brain and Attachment Style Can Help You Defuse Conflict and Build a Secure Relationship* (Oakland, CA: New Harbinger, 2012).

4. Levine and Heller, *Attached*, 177–182.

5. Rick Hanson, FACES Conference, San Diego, May 2015.

6. Gary Chapman, *The 5 Love Languages: The Secret to Love That Lasts,* repr. ed. (Chicago: Northfield Publishing, 2015).

7. Dan Siegel, "Wheel of Awareness," accessed September 4, 2018, drdansiegel.com/resources/wheel_of_awareness/.

Chapter Four: Disorganized Attachment

1. Dan Siegel, *The Developing Mind: How Relationships and the Brain Interact to Shape Who We Are,* 2nd ed. (New York: Guilford Press, 2012); Sarah Jenkins, "Trauma and Dissociation: Beyond Your 'Window of Tolerance,'" GoodTherapy (blog), Jun 23, 2016, goodtherapy.org/blog/trauma-dissociation-beyond-your-window-of-tolerance-0623165.

2. "Disorganized Attachment: How Disorganized Attachments Form & How They Can Be Healed," Psych Alive, accessed September 19, 2018, psychalive.org/disorganized-attachment.

3. Peter Payne, Peter A. Levine, and Mardi A. Crane-Goudreau, "Somatic experiencing: using interoception and proprioception as core elements of trauma therapy," *Frontiers in Psychology*, February 4, 2015, frontiersin.org/articles/10.3389/fpsyg.2015.00093/full.

4. Peter Levine, Stephen Porges, and Maggie Phillips, "Healing Trauma and Pain Through Polyvagal Science and Its Interlocking Somatic Interventions," accessed September 4, 2018, maggiephillipsphd.com/Polyvagal/EBookHealingTraumaPainThroughPolyvagalScience.pdf

5. Stephen Porges, "The Polyvagal Theory with Stephen Porges, PhD," interview by David Van Nuys, *Shrink Rap Radio* no. 265, June 3, 2011, shrinkrapradio.com/265.pdf.

6. Rachel Hosie, "How Personal Space Boundaries Vary in Different Countries," *Independent*, May 2, 2017, independent.co.uk/life-style/personal-space-boundaries-different-countries-argentina-uk-romania-a7713051.html.

7. Patti Wood, *Snap: Making the Most of First Impressions, Body Language, and Charisma* (Novato, CA: New World Library, 2012).

8. David Wallin, "Because Connection Takes Two: the Analyst's Psychology in Treating the 'Connection Resistant' Patient," *International Journal of Psychoanalytic Self-Psychology* 9, no. 3 (2014): 200–207, doi.org/10.1080/15551024.2014.917460.

Chapter Five: Attachment Styles and Romantic Partnerships

1. Stan Tatkin, "Find Your Mentor Couple" (blog post), 2013, stantatkinblog.wordpress.com/2012/12/27/find-your-mentor-couple/.

2. Kim John Payne and Diane Poole Heller, *Secure Attachment Parenting in the Digital Age: Neuroscience, Technology & the Next Generation* (webinar series), originally released November 6, 2017, attachmentmastery.com/parenting/.

3. Amir Levine, "Deciphering Attachment Styles in Everyday Life for Dating and Relationships" (keynote address), April 9, 2016, DARe to Connect: Attachment, Trauma & Intimacy Conference, Boulder, CO.

4. Stan Tatkin, "Does Your Relationship Come First? The Secrets of Secure Functioning Relationships" (keynote address), April 8, 2017, DARe to Connect: Attachment, Trauma & Intimacy Conference, Boulder, CO.

5. Stan Tatkin, *Wired for Love: How Understanding Your Partner's Brain and Attachment Style Can Help You Defuse Conflict and Build a Secure Relationship* (Oakland, CA: New Harbinger, 2012).

6. Tatkin, *Wired for Love.*

7. Amir Levine and Rachel Heller, *Attached: The New Science of Adult Attachment and How It Can Help You Find—and Keep—Love* (New York: TarcherPerigee, 2012), 11.

8. Stan Tatkin, *Wired for Dating: How Understanding Neurobiology and Attachment Style Can Help You Find Your Ideal Mate* (Oakland, CA: New Harbinger, 2016).

9. Levine and Heller, *Attached*, 136–137, 235–236, 245–251.

10. John Bowlby, *Attachment and Loss, Volume Two (Separation: Anxiety and Anger)* (New York: Basic Books, 1973); Cindy Hazan and Phillip Shaver, "Romantic Love Conceptualized as an Attachment Process," *Journal of Personality and Social Psychology* 52, no. 3 (March 1987): 511–24, pdfs.semanticscholar.org/a7ed/78521d0d3a52b6ce532e89ce6ba185b355c3.pdf.

11. Levine and Heller, *Attached*, 52–54. 100–101, 116–117, 120–122, 161 (avoidant); 57–59, 81, 160–162 (Anxious/Ambivalent).

12. Rick Hanson and Richard Mendius, *Buddha's Brain: The Practical Neuroscience of Happiness, Love, and Wisdom* (Oakland, CA: New Harbinger, 2009), 67–77.

13. Levine and Heller, *Attached*, 160–162, 190–193, 206–207.

SELECTED BIBLIOGRAPHY

All of us working in this field owe so much to those who have come before us and laid the ground for our efforts. We also owe an ongoing debt to our peers, whose work informs and betters our own. If you're interested in learning more about secure attachment or any of the related fields I've incorporated into my work, I strongly suggest the following list of brilliant authors, researchers, and therapists—most of whom I've already mentioned in the preceding chapters. I hope it goes without saying that this book would not be possible without the hard work of these wonderful people.

Ainsworth, Mary D. Salter. *Infancy in Uganda: Infant Care and the Growth of Love.* Baltimore: Johns Hopkins Press, 1967.

Ainsworth, Mary D. Salter, Mary C. Blehar, Everett Waters, and Sally N. Wall. *Patterns of Attachment: A Psychological Study of the Strange Situation.* New York: Psychology Press, 2015.

Badenoch, Bonnie. *Being a Brain-Wise Therapist: A Practical Guide to Interpersonal Neurobiology.* New York: Norton, 2008.

———. *The Heart of Trauma: Healing the Embodied Brain in the Context of Relationships.* New York: Norton, 2014.

Bader, Ellyn, and Peter Pearson. *In Quest of the Mythical Mate: A Developmental Approach to Diagnosis and Treatment in Couples Therapy.* Abingdon, UK: Routledge, 2014.

———. *Tell Me No Lies: How to Stop Lying to Your Partner—and Yourself—in the 4 Stages of Marriage.* New York: St. Martins, 2001.

Beebe, Beatrice, Phyllis Cohen, and Frank Lachmann. *The Mother-Infant Interaction Picture Book: Origins of Attachment.* New York: Norton, 2016.

Beebe, Beatrice, Phyllis Cohen, K. Mark Sossin, and Sara Markese, eds. *Mothers, Infants, and Children of September 11, 2001: A Primary Prevention Project.* Abingdon, UK: Routledge, 2012.

Beebe, Beatrice, and Frank Lachmann. *The Origins of Attachment: Infant Research and Adult Treatment.* Abingdon, UK: Routledge, 2013.

Bentzen, Marianne. *The Neuroaffective Picture Book: An Illustrated Introduction to Developmental Neuropsychology.* Berkeley, CA: North Atlantic Books, 2018.

——. *Through Windows of Opportunity: A Neuroaffective Approach to Child Psychotherapy.* Abingdon, UK: Routledge, 2015.

Bowlby, John. *Attachment and Loss: Volume One (Attachment).* New York: Basic Books, 1969.

——. *Attachment and Loss: Volume Two (Separation: Anxiety and Anger).* New York: Basic Books, 1973.

——. *Attachment and Loss: Volume Three (Loss: Sadness and Depression).* New York: Basic Books, 1980.

——. *The Making and Breaking of Affectional Bonds.* Abingdon, UK: Routledge, 2005.

——. *A Secure Base: Parent-Child Attachment and Healthy Human Development.* New York: Basic Books, 1988.

Bowlby, John, Margery Fry, and Mary D. Salter Ainsworth. *Child Care and the Growth of Love.* London: Penguin, 1953.

Chapman, Gary. *The 5 Love Languages: The Secret to Love that Lasts.* Chicago: Northfield, 2015.

——. *Loving Your Spouse When You Feel Like Walking Away: Real Help for Desperate Hearts in Difficult Marriages.* Chicago: Northfield, 2018.

——. *Things I Wish I'd Known Before We Got Married.* Chicago: Northfield, 2010.

Chitty, John. *Working with Babies: A Five-Part Therapy Method for Infants and Their Families.* Ithaca, NY: CSES, 2016.

Ecker, Bruce, Robin Ticic, and Laurel Hulley. *Unlocking the Emotional Brain: Eliminating Symptoms at Their Roots Using Memory Reconsolidation.* New York: Routledge, 2012.

Ferentz, Lisa. *Finding Your Ruby Slippers: Transformative Life Lessons from the Therapist's Couch.* Eau Claire, WI: PESI, 2017.

———. *.Letting Go of Self-Destructive Behaviors: A Workbook of Hope and Healing.* Abingdon, UK: Routledge, 2014.

———. *Treating Self-Destructive Behaviors in Trauma Survivors: A Clinician's Guide.* Abingdon, UK: Routledge, 2014.

Fonagy, Peter. *Attachment Theory and Psychoanalysis.* New York: Other Press, 2001.

Frederickson, Barbara. *Love 2.0: Finding Happiness and Health in Moments of Connection.* New York: Plume, 2013.

———. *Positivity: Top-Notch Research Reveals the 3 to 1 Ratio That Will Change Your Life.* New York: Three Rivers, 2009.

Gojman-de-Millan, Sonia, Christian Herreman, and L. Alan Sroufe, eds. *Attachment Across Clinical and Cultural Perspectives: A Relational Psychoanalytic Approach.* Abingdon, UK: Routledge, 2016.

Goldbart, Stephen, and David Wallin. *Mapping the Terrain of the Heart: Passion, Tenderness, and the Capacity to Love.* Northvale, NJ: Jason Aronson, 1998.

Goleman, Daniel. *Emotional Intelligence: Why It Can Matter More Than IQ.* New York: Bantam, 2005.

Gottman, John, and Joan DeClaire. *The Relationship Cure: A 5 Step Guide to Strengthening Your Marriage, Family, and Friendships.* New York: Harmony, 2002.

Gottman, John, and Nan Silver. *The Seven Principles for Making Marriage Work: A Practical Guide from the Country's Foremost Relationship Expert.* New York: Harmony, 2015.

———. *What Makes Love Last? How to Build Trust and Avoid Betrayal.* New York: Simon and Schuster, 2013.

Grand, David. *Brainspotting: The Revolutionary New Therapy for Rapid and Effective Change.* Boulder, CO: Sounds True, 2013.

——. *Emotional Healing at Warp Speed: The Power of EMDR.* New York: Harmony, 2001.

Greenfield, Patricia Marks, and Edward Tronick. *Infant Curriculum.* Pacific Palisades, CA: Goodyear Publishing, 1980.

Hanson, Rick. *Buddha's Brain: The Practical Neuroscience of Happiness, Love, and Wisdom.* Oakland, CA: New Harbinger, 2009.

——. *Hardwiring Happiness: The New Brain Science of Contentment, Calm, and Confidence.* New York: Harmony, 2013.

——. *Just One Thing: Developing a Buddha Brain One Simple Practice at a Time.* Oakland, CA: New Harbinger, 2011.

Hart, Susan. *Brain, Attachment, Personality: An Introduction to Neuroaffective Development.* Abingdon, UK: Routledge, 2018.

——. *The Impact of Attachment.* New York: Norton, 2010.

Hart, Susan, and Mary Campa, eds. *Human Bonding: The Science of Affectional Ties.* New York: Guilford Press, 2013.

Heller, Laurence, and Aline LaPierre. *Healing Developmental Trauma: How Early Trauma Affects Self-Regulation, Self-Image, and the Capacity for Relationship.* Berkeley, CA: North Atlantic Books, 2012.

Johnson, Sue. *Hold Me Tight: Seven Conversations for a Lifetime of Love.* New York: Little, Brown, 2008.

——. *Love Sense: The Revolutionary New Science of Romantic Relationships.* New York: Little, Brown, 2013.

Kaplan, Louise. *Adolescence: The Farewell to Childhood.* New York: Simon & Schuster, 1984.

——. *No Voice Is Ever Wholly Lost: An Exploration of the Everlasting Attachment Between Parent and Child.* New York: Simon & Schuster, 1996.

——. *Oneness and Separateness: From Infant to Individual.* New York: Simon & Schuster, 1998.

Levine, Amir, and Rachel Heller. *Attached: The New Science of Adult Attachment and How It Can Help You Find—and Keep—Love.* New York: TarcherPerigee, 2012.

Levine, Peter. *Healing Trauma: A Pioneering Program for Restoring the Wisdom of Your Body.* Boulder, CO: Sounds True, 2008.

——. *In an Unspoken Voice: How the Body Releases Trauma and Restores Goodness.* Berkeley, CA: North Atlantic Books, 2010.

Levine, Peter, with Ann Frederick. *Waking the Tiger: Healing Trauma.* Berkeley, CA: North Atlantic Books, 1997.

Levine, Peter, and Maggie Kline. *Trauma-Proofing Your Kids: A Parent's Guide for Instilling Confidence, Joy and Resilience.* Berkeley, CA: North Atlantic Books, 2008.

Love, Patricia. *The Truth About Love: The Highs, the Lows, and How You Can Make It Last Forever.* New York: Fireside, 2001.

Love, Patricia, and Jo Robinson. *Hot Monogamy: Essential Steps to More Passionate, Intimate Lovemaking.* Scotts Valley, CA: Create Space, 2012.

Maté, Gabor. *In the Realm of Hungry Ghosts: Close Encounters with Addiction.* Berkeley, CA: North Atlantic Books, 2010.

——. *When the Body Says No: The Cost of Hidden Stress.* Toronto: Vintage Canada, 2004.

Napier, Nancy. *Getting Through the Day: Strategies for Adults Hurt as Children.* New York: Norton, 1994.

——. *Recreating Your Self: Building Self-Esteem through Imaging and Self-Hypnosis.* New York: Norton, 1996.

——. *Sacred Practices for Conscious Living.* New York, Norton, 1997.

Ogden, Pat, and Janina Fisher. *Sensorimotor Psychotherapy: Interventions for Trauma and Attachment.* New York: Norton, 2015.

Ogden, Pat, Kekuni Minton, and Clare Pain. *Trauma and the Body: A Sensorimotor Approach to Psychotherapy.* New York: Norton, 2006.

O'Hanlon, Bill. *Do One Thing Different: Ten Simple Ways to Change Your Life.* New York: William Morrow, 1999.

———. *Out of the Blue: Six Non-Medication Ways to Relieve Depression.* New York, Norton, 2014.

———. *Quick Steps to Resolving Trauma.* New York, Norton, 2010.

Payne, Kim John. *The Soul of Discipline: The Simplicity Parenting Approach to Warm, Firm, and Calm Guidance—From Toddlers to Teens.* New York: Ballantine, 2015.

Payne, Kim John, with Lisa Ross. *Simplicity Parenting: Using the Extraordinary Power of Less to Raise Calmer, Happier, and More Secure Kids.* New York: Ballantine, 2010.

Piaget, Jean. *Play, Dreams, and Imitation in Childhood.* Translated by C. Gattegno and F.M. Hodgson. New York, Norton, 1962.

———. *The Moral Judgment of the Child.* Translated by Marjorie Gabain. New York: Free Press, 1997.

Piaget, Jean, and Bärbel Inhelder. *The Psychology of the Child.* Translated by Helen Weaver. New York: Basic Books 1969.

Porges, Stephen. *The Polyvagal Theory: Neurophysiological Foundations of Emotions, Attachment, Communication, and Self-Regulation.* New York: Norton, 2011.

Rapson, James, and Craig English. *Anxious to Please: 7 Revolutionary Practices for the Chronically Nice.* Naperville, IL: Sourcebooks, 2006.

Real, Terrence. *How Can I Get Through to You? Closing the Intimacy Gap Between Men and Women.* New York: Fireside, 2002.

———. *The New Rules of Marriage: What You Need to Know to Make Love Work.* New York: Ballantine, 2008.

Rhimes, Shonda. *Year of Yes: How to Dance It Out, Stand in the Sun and Be Your Own Person.* New York: Simon & Schuster, 2015.

Rothenberg, Mira. *Children with Emerald Eyes: Histories of Extraordinary Boys and Girls.* Berkeley, CA: North Atlantic Books, 2003.

Rothschild, Babette. *The Body Remembers: The Psychophysiology of Trauma and Trauma Treatment.* New York: Norton, 2000.

———. *8 Keys to Safe Trauma Recovery: Take-Charge Strategies to Empower Your Healing.* New York: Norton, 2010.

——. *Trauma Essentials: The Go-To Guide.* New York: Norton, 2011.

Scaer, Robert. *The Body Bears the Burden: Trauma, Dissociation, and Disease.* Abingdon, UK: Routledge, 2014.

——. *The Trauma Spectrum: Hidden Wounds and Human Resiliency.* New York: Norton, 2005.

Schwartz, Richard. *Internal Family Systems Therapy.* New York: Guilford Press, 1997.

——. *Introduction to the Internal Family Systems Model.* Oak Park, IL: Trailheads, 2001.

Siegel, Daniel. *The Developing Mind: How Relationships and the Brain Interact to Shape Who We Are.* New York: Guilford Press, 2001.

Siegel, Daniel, and Tina Payne Bryson. *The Whole-Brain Child: 12 Revolutionary Strategies to Nurture Your Child's Developing Mind.* New York: Bantam, 2012.

——. *The Yes Brain: How to Cultivate Courage, Curiosity, and Resilience in Your Child.* New York: Bantam, 2018.

Siegel, Daniel, and Mary Hartzell. *Parenting from the Inside Out: How a Deeper Self-Understanding Can Help You Raise Children Who Thrive.* New York: Penguin, 2013.

Sroufe, L. Alan. *Emotional Development: The Organization of Emotional Life in the Early Years.* Cambridge: Cambridge University Press, 1995.

Tatkin, Stan. *We Do: Saying Yes to a Relationship of Depth, True Connection, and Enduring Love.* Boulder, CO: Sounds True, 2018.

——. *Wired for Dating: How Understanding Neurobiology and Attachment Style Can Help You Find Your Ideal Mate.* Oakland, CA: New Harbinger, 2016.

——. *Wired for Love: How Understanding Your Partner's Brain and Attachment Style Can Help You Defuse Conflict and Build a Secure Relationship.* Oakland, CA: New Harbinger, 2012.

Tronick, Edward. *Babies as People.* New York: Collier Books, 1980.

———. *The Neurobehavioral and Social-Emotional Development of Infants and Children.* New York: Norton, 2007.

van der Kolk, Bessel. *The Body Keeps the Score: Brain, Mind, and Body in the Healing of Trauma.* New York: Penguin, 2014.

Wallin, David. *Attachment in Psychotherapy.* New York: Guilford Press, 2015.

Wood, Patti. *Snap: Making the Most of First Impressions, Body Language, and Charisma.* Novato, CA: New World Library, 2012.

Zayas, Vivian, and Cindy Hazan, eds. *Bases of Adult Attachment: Linking Brain, Mind and Behavior.* New York: Springer, 2015.

INDEX

childhood (*continued*)
memories of, 2
object permanence and, 92
on-and-off attachment and, 82–83
secure attachment and, 13
signal cry and, 91
trauma and, 100

children, 114. *See also* infants
absent caregivers and, 59
adaptation by, 17–18, 57–58, 59, 60
attachment styles and, 112–13,
146–48 (*see also* childhood; *specific attachment styles*)
avoidant attachment and, 57–58,
59, 60
caregivers and, 9, 13, 47–50, 58–60,
64, 83–86, 109, 113, 147, 168
(*see also* neglect)
communicating with, 134
disrupted engagement and, 60
emotional needs of, 59, 68–69, 168
emotional neglect of, 68–69
expressive dissonance and, 59–60
eye contact and, 41, 64–65
interrupted regulation and, 83–84
isolation and, 59
neglected, 13, 60, 85 (*see also* neglect)
overstimulation and, 84–85, 108
in prosocial families, 9
proximity seeking and, 86
in regulating environment, 7
rejection of, 60
repairing relationships with, 44
reversing role reversal and, 47–50
secure attachment and, 28–31
"skin hunger" and, 59
stress and, 82–83
task-based presence and, 59
temperment and, 147
unpredictable caregivers and, 13–14

clinginess, 86. *See also* proximity seeking

closeness, 30, 61, 64, 77, 95, 153,
156, 162, 174–75. *See also* connection(s); intimacy

cognitive development, attachment
theory and, 16–19

cognitive empathy, 37

"co-mindfulness," 8

comings and goings, being mindful of
(SAS# 6), 39–42

commitment, mutual, 150

communicating simply and clearly, 134

communication. *See also* signal cry
with children, 134
confusing, 115–16
nonverbal, 152–53, 161 (*see also* eye contact)
verbal, 152, 161

compassion, 2, 4, 149

competent protector (exercise), 116–19

conflicts, 174
conflict resolution, 153–54
considering, 160

confusion, 125–26

connection(s), 3, 6, 12, 32, 37, 42, 61,
66, 77, 125, 151, 156, 169. *See also* intimacy
broken, 3, 5, 146
maintaining through disagreement,
153–54
restoring, 3, 101–4
stable, 154
stress of, 63

consistent and predictable people
(exercise), 93

contact, maintaining (SAS #5), 38–39

contingency, 10–12
recalling (exercise), 12

control, loss of, 5, 88, 146

controlling behaviors, 123–24, 142,
153

co-regulation, 6–8, 9–10, 83, 109, 151

critique, 65, 69, 92

Dear Sounds True friend,

Since 1985, Sounds True has been sharing spiritual wisdom and resources to help people live more genuine, loving, and fulfilling lives. We hope that our programs inspire and uplift you, enabling you to bring forth your unique voice and talents for the benefit of us all.

We would like to invite you to become part of our growing online community by giving you three downloadable programs— an introduction to the treasure of authors and artists available at Sounds True! To receive these gifts, just flip this card over for details, then visit us at **SoundsTrue.com/Free** and enter your email for instant access.

With love on the journey,

TAMI SIMON   Founder and Publisher, Sounds True

many voices, one journey   800.333.9185

ST330

ABOUT THE AUTHOR

Diane Poole Heller, PhD, is an established expert in the field of child and adult attachment theory and models, trauma resolution, and integrative healing techniques. She developed her own signature series on adult attachment called DARe (Dynamic Attachment Re-patterning experience), also known as SATe (Somatic Attachment Training experience), which is now taught to therapists around the globe. Diane began her work with Peter Levine, founder of the Somatic Experiencing® Trauma Institute (SETI) in 1989, going on to teach Somatic Experiencing (SE) internationally for over twenty years and becoming a senior faculty member at SETI.

A dynamic teacher and speaker, Diane has also authored several articles in her fields of interest. Her book *Crash Course: A Self-Healing Guide to Auto Accident Trauma and Recovery* is used worldwide as a resource for healing a variety of overwhelming life events. Her film *Surviving Columbine* aired on CNN and supported community healing in the aftermath of the school shootings. Her popular audio program, *Healing Your Attachment Wounds: How to Create Deep and Lasting Intimate Relationships*, was released by Sounds True in 2018.

As president of Trauma Solutions, an organization that trains psychotherapists, Diane works diligently to support the professional helping community. She maintains a limited private practice in Louisville, Colorado. Find out more about Diane and her work at **dianepooleheller.com.**

ABOUT SOUNDS TRUE

Sounds True is a multimedia publisher whose mission is to inspire and support personal transformation and spiritual awakening. Founded in 1985 and located in Boulder, Colorado, we work with many of the leading spiritual teachers, thinkers, healers, and visionary artists of our time. We strive with every title to preserve the essential "living wisdom" of the author or artist. It is our goal to create products that not only provide information to a reader or listener, but that also embody the quality of a wisdom transmission.

For those seeking genuine transformation, Sounds True is your trusted partner. At SoundsTrue.com you will find a wealth of free resources to support your journey, including exclusive weekly audio interviews, free downloads, interactive learning tools, and other special savings on all our titles.

To learn more, please visit SoundsTrue.com/freegifts or call us toll-free at 800.333.9185.

sounds true
WAKING UP THE WORLD